What Google Cannot Teach

EDUCATION OF THE HEART AND MIND

ARJUN RAY

INDIA • SINGAPORE • MALAYSIA

Notion Press

Old No. 38, New No. 6
McNichols Road, Chetpet
Chennai - 600 031

First Published by Notion Press 2019
Copyright © Arjun Ray 2019
All Rights Reserved.

ISBN 978-1-64587-623-6

This book has been published with all efforts taken to make the material error-free after the consent of the author. However, the author and the publisher do not assume and hereby disclaim any liability to any party for any loss, damage, or disruption caused by errors or omissions, whether such errors or omissions result from negligence, accident, or any other cause.

While every effort has been made to avoid any mistake or omission, this publication is being sold on the condition and understanding that neither the author nor the publishers or printers would be liable in any manner to any person by reason of any mistake or omission in this publication or for any action taken or omitted to be taken or advice rendered or accepted on the basis of this work. For any defect in printing or binding the publishers will be liable only to replace the defective copy by another copy of this work then available.

Contents

Preface 5

Acknowledgements 13

Introduction: What Google Cannot Teach 15

1. Purpose and Meaning to Life 25
2. Personal Vision 46
3. Unlocking Human Potential 58
4. Lifelong Learning 71
5. The Renaissance in Innovation 84
6. Learning to Lead 102
7. Measuring the Impact of Leadership 123
8. Goal-Setting 137
9. Deep Reading, Deep Thinking, Deep Learning 152
10. Reflective Thinking 173
11. Where the Mind Is without Fear 184
12. Psychological Robustness 195

Afterword – What Google Should Teach 207

Preface

Soon after the Kargil War of 1999, I assumed command of the newly created 14 Corps in Ladakh in June 2000. Incipient insurgency was staring us in the face, and had started spilling over from the Kashmir Valley and from across Pakistan Occupied Baltistan into Kargil District. Our greatest concern was the alienation of the local populace. This can be judged by the fact that before the start of the Kargil War, no local person came forth to tell us, that Pakistani regulars had intruded in strength, over a large swathe of Indian Territory.

While appreciating the security situation of a region, intelligence agencies are often overly influenced by the number and intensity of acts of terror. They seldom gauge the alienation levels of the people; which can be the oxygen terrorism needs, to survive. Terrorism cannot survive without popular support. Development without human security is meaningless. Building infrastructure and giving jobs is not enough; the people need to feel trusted and emotionally and physically secure. They need to be assimilated into the mainstream as proof of trust. Not understanding these fundamental truths is responsible for the thousands of innocent people who are dying every day in all the terror spots of the world.

This is what is meant by human security. This is what we successfully achieved – through Operation *Sadbhavna* (Goodwill), a massive socio-political campaign, to win over alienated communities. For the past seventeen years there has been complete peace in Ladakh and the people are patriotic Indians, like any other citizen in the country. This brings us to the second great lesson in leadership and insurgency: winning the hearts and minds battle is a shibboleth. You have to first win the hearts of the people before their minds can be won over. To win their hearts is to win their trust; only thereafter will development make sense.

For me, *Sadbhavna* was a crucible experience. Above all, I realized that the purpose of life cannot be to be rich, famous or powerful; man must have a higher purpose; it is this purpose that gives meaning to his life. The purpose is transcendental, in that, it is for someone other than man himself or those who are close to him. Motivated with this spiritual lesson of life, I decided to retire prematurely after serving the army for just over 37 years; flew into Bangalore the very next day; and started setting up the Indus International School.

After achieving a challenging goal of winning peace and wiping out insurgency without using guns and bullets, a seemingly impossible possibility, I had to reinvent myself, by setting another challenging goal. I realized that if I did not, I would find myself in the depressive condition which Apollo 11 astronauts Buzz Aldrin and Neil Armstrong experienced, after their return from walking on the moon. There was a deep vacuum in their bodies and minds – emptiness that led to anonymity.

The more I reflected, the more I was convinced about the strategic role of education in the 21st century in a future driven by Artificial Intelligence and machine-thinking, characterized by volatility, complexity and uncertainty. My purpose started taking shape around the big idea: *Future competition between nations and individuals will not be between competing political ideologies or competing economic systems.* Future competition will be between competing education systems. Education and the Internet are making the world flat; a level playing field.

We see what education has done to the United States. The shocking reality that Donald Trump is the 45th American President is a severe indictment of the country's education system. Even if Donald Trump fails his Presidency, the long-term solution will be to fix the education system, a system that has created millions of literate Americans who want Trump as their leader, a person who disrespects women, is racist and religiously intolerant, exhibits gross consumerism, and is unashamedly proud of his sexual prowess.

The next breakthrough in my thinking came by selecting international education over the national curriculum. My logic proceeded as follows. The traditional education system based on rote-memorization and success in examinations, was unsuited to preparing students to deal with uncertainty and fierce competition in a globalized world. The global challenge of sustainability could only be ensured by innovation, and by leaders who possessed life competencies of critical thinking, big-picture thinking, lifelong learning skills, collaboration, the values of empathy, compassion, reverence for life, and persuasive communication skills. This was and still is my understanding of academic rigour in the 21st century – a combination of academic excellence and life competencies.

The Indus River flows through Leh, the capital of Ladakh, which was my military headquarters. The river inspired me as it identifies India. It meanders along its course through China, India and Pakistan into the Arabian Sea; another symbol of the idea of global citizenship, though not at the cost of one's local identity. In my thinking, localism is a prerequisite for globalism. The banks of this great river were the obvious choice for me to sit, reflect and write out the vision of today's Indus Schools.

> *"To create global citizens and leaders of tomorrow, through traditional values of love, empathy, discipline and respect – 21st Century citizens who think globally and act locally."*

Armed with this vision I came to Bangalore to start an international school. The vision remains unchanged!

This book is not exclusively about international education, or teachers and schools, or even a chain of schools. It is about the school of life in how to find fulfilling work, how to unlock one's potential, how to succeed through passion and effort, and how to be happy. In our interconnected world we must look upon education not as schooling or college going; but lifelong learning about oneself and about life. Our preparation for life is continuous; never complete; every day is a day for unlearning and relearning. Learning, teaching, leading and innovation are indivisible. This book is, therefore, meant for anyone who wants to be a lifelong learner and an innovator.

The purpose of writing this book flows out of my desire to institutionalize leadership and innovation. Although the international school has been chosen as a working model, it is equally relevant in the private, public and social space for all organizations and institutions. It is based on 38 years' experience of military service and 17 years as head of India's best international schools – Bangalore, Hyderabad and Pune. My thoughts are shared with leaders, educationists, teachers, students and even parents. The objective that I share with such people is that, our schools become vibrant and inspirational learning organizations, which engage and motivate a whole new generation of young people to reclaim, repair and restore what is good in their native countries and cultures. This can be achieved only with the right kind of leadership, which requires courage and expertise to meet all challenges of time, place and context.

I am conscious of the fact that warfare and conflict are too serious a subject be left to Generals. Likewise, school reforms to design the future are too serious a mission to be left to teachers alone. Everyone has to be involved, from politicians, to bureaucrats, to corporate leaders and private citizens. They are all stakeholders.

But there is a serious challenge that lies in the path to modernization and reform – teachers. Transformation at the cutting edge, the school, cannot happen unless teachers are entrepreneurial – innovative and risk-takers, and are ready to move out of their comfort zones. As a community, teachers the world over are not entrepreneurial. They are protagonists for status quo. This explains why in the past 225 years, the basic structure of schooling has not changed. It is all brick and mortar, both inside and outside the classroom.

This book is about the urgent need to transform teachers into smart creatives and recommend that there is a need to develop an interdisciplinary culture amongst teachers. This would include a fair proportion of lateral induction of non-teaching professionals into schools. Such a move will hopefully usher in avant-garde teacherpreneurs who are visionary, innovative and interdisciplinary.

There are over 90,000 books on leadership and self-help, and nearly 95 percent of them have been written by non-practitioners of leadership; mainly academics and consultants who hold forth on leadership and management, research scholars, psychologists, journalists and social scientists. Likewise, most reputed books on education have been written by "teacher experts" and professors from renowned universities. They lack "boots-on-the-ground" experience, and are woefully short on interdisciplinary expertise.

Despite the Internet revolution, teacher effectiveness is still being judged on knowledge of content, pedagogy and teacher disposition, in that order. Google has turned this priority on its head. The changed priority is disposition, pedagogy and content; in that order. Content is no longer subject expertise, but includes everything that is interconnected knowledge.

The purpose of education, the purpose of man, and role of the 21st century teacher is the same – to unlock one's potential in order to be self-aware, happy and prepared for all challenges.

Motivation to gain higher education in the West must be supported by mass education of all who seek to study abroad, that they will have opportunities to return to their countries of origin, opportunities not just based on patriotism and charity. Use of their skills acquired abroad can be used in their own countries. Moreover, they can enrich national expertise in several areas and earn decently as well.

Most students in Asia-Pacific region and Africa head for the best universities in the Western world, never to return to their homeland. In a macro sense, international education seems to be encouraging intellectual migration. A key aspect of international education is localism and sustainability. Good education must reconnect a child with his country, his culture and people, and motivate students to plough back their wealth, experience, and talent to make their society sustainable. We call this payback time; this is the decanted essence of sustainability:

Sustainable man.

Sustainable family.

Sustainable community.

Sustainable country.

Sustainable world.

This book is an edited transcription of selected lectures and presentations made to schools, teachers and students of Indus schools. The central idea of these lectures was transformational leadership: unlocking human potential, preparation for life's journey into an uncertain and turbulent world ahead, and leaving behind an institutional legacy of leadership, innovation and strong faculty.

The underlying premise at Indus is that the role of the great teacher is to unlock her potential first, and then that of her students, by teaching what Google cannot teach. To unlock potential is a creative act, an act of supreme innovation. This book is about transformational leadership because great leaders are teachers and great teachers are leaders. Teachers and leaders share two common goals – unlocking human potential, and self-actualization as a prerequisite for professional development. This is the central perspective of the book: and is therefore relevant for leaders who could be teaching in classrooms; leading multinational corporations; governing civil society; and students in school, at work, in life.

All leaders share a collective ambition. Once we retire from active service and muse over the golden yesterdays, we will not remember the profits we made to the company, the honours and accolades we received, or the academic scores that enabled students gain entry into the prestigious colleges and universities. We will remember only those people we developed as leaders from tomorrow. The only three million dollar questions we need to answer are: How are the people you were once responsible for doing today? Did you develop leaders? Did you share your teachable points of view?

Acknowledgements

This book is based on several lectures I have given to teachers, students and parents of our schools. My premise right through has been that, purpose, and self-actualization are pre-conditions for education of the heart and mind to prepare children for life, for a future we do not know, and for jobs that don't exist today.

I owe a lot to everyone who helped me spread my ideas. I am indebted to them for their unflinching support and feedback.

At Indus, I wish to thank Sarojini Rao, the Principal of Indus Bangalore, for sharing her successful experiences as one of the best school principals in India. In addition to being an excellent sounding board, her practical suggestions in teacher reform were invaluable.

I owe a lot to my oldest and dearest friend for over 65 years, Ranjeet Chordia, one of the finest brains I have come across. He can be the devil's advocate with the ability of calling a spade and shovel. I am forever thankful to him for forcing me to re-examine various issues from different perspectives.

My gratitude goes to Mrs PB Benjamin, Bangalore's well-known educationist, for meticulous editing and highlighting the finer nuances of teacher and child mentality.

My thanks to my personal assistant, Suresha M, by his unfailing support in spending hours of sweat and toil to prepare several drafts before they saw the light of day.

Most of all my gratitude goes out to Saroj, who encouraged me to write and gave me the right space and opportunities to balance work and home life. This involved a lot of sacrifice in family time, a price I was able to pay. Her constant support and understanding made this possible.

Introduction: What Google Cannot Teach

Google has changed the world, the market, the way we work and study, our relationships, and our lives. We can navigate our lives and work, using the Google search engine. Google is the grand-parent, the nanny and even our personal doctor. However, when we type in *what Google cannot teach*, we receive no satisfactory acknowledgements on the Internet. Even related searches give no convincing answers. The odd response makes a reference to some inconsequential feedback, such as; *internet cannot teach: grit*. The Internet cannot give any instructions on what one should do in the future, what one needs to pay attention to in the present, and what is really important for one-self.

In schools, Google has high-jacked the arena of presenting content for students, leaving the teacher somewhat out in the cold. With nearly 80 percent of content available on the Internet, the teacher is no longer the sole repository of knowledge. Google has enabled students to be self-directed learners, to be their own teachers. It is the 20 percent of a curriculum that Google cannot teach, and this position is unlikely to change in the foreseeable future.

Google is aware of this imbalance and is determined to redress the situation. The giant search engine launched a secret project in 2011, *Google Brain,* in collaboration with Stanford University and other Google researchers to develop artificial intelligence for deep learning. The *Google Brain* is expected to be an artificial brain, driven probably by DNA computers using human protein strands as biological chips.

When this happens, Ray Kurzweil's prophecy may come true: the arrival of the age of singularity, of Homo Deus, when consciousness will be implanted in an artificial being; the day when the laws of biology will no longer be relevant, and human beings will cease to be what they are today.

Ray Kurzweil and the *Google Brain* team are hopeful that they will be able to reverse engineer the brain, and gain deeper insight into who we are and what the purpose of life is. Should this come about, Google is likely to change its identity, from a search engine to a machine-learning company. Present forecasts are optimistic that this may become a reality by 2030, despite Professor Stephen Hawking's concern that, "*The development of full artificial intelligence could spell the end of the human race.*" This warning cannot be taken lightly, as thus far the human race has been handicapped by the slow speed of its evolution.

When will the age of singularity arrive, if at all, is anyone's guess. But should this happen, Google may be able to replicate the brain; not the mind. *Google Brain* may then be able to teach 90 percent of what is presently taught in classrooms. Notwithstanding this spectacular scientific achievement, the remaining 10 percent will still outweigh the benefits of the machine brain because machines lack consciousness.

"Google cannot replace the primacy of man over machine."

The techno-giants of the 21st century – Google, Apple, Amazon, Microsoft and Facebook are reversing the history of man, from Homo Sapiens to Homo Deus. The scenario is straight out of sci fi movies. They are not speculative nor are they a narrative about alternative worlds – it is happening in our life time. Now.

The Googles of Silicon Valley and Seattle are building "AI complete" companies, to create machines that can out-think human beings, and surpass human intelligence in a world driven by algorithms and machine-thinking. They are desperately and even successfully, to some extent, ushering the age of rationality and order, wherein engineers will be expected to replace politicians.

Most importantly, the five tech-giants are in the business of knowledge monopoly, threatening our individuality. We are silently witnessing, and sadly, even endorsing, the death of the heroic individual and, of human creativity. In medieval Europe, creativity was regarded as an act of divinity, and we are familiar with how Thomas Aquinas summed up this belief: "*God alone creates.*"

A few centuries later, around the middle of the 20th century, Ayn Rand redefined the genesis of creativity and the greatness of the *heroic individual*:

> "*My philosophy in essence, is the concept of man as a heroic being, with his own happiness as the moral purpose of his life, with productive achievement as his noblest activity, and reason as his only absolute.*"

The Silicon Valley view is different and disturbing, and is likely to have irreversible implications on the greatest spiritual idea in all religions: who am I? The Silicon Valley view is that creativity is a byproduct of collaboration; that great teams produce better and more creative ideas. The examples are there for us to see.

- Google's ranking of websites and Amazon's algorithms are based on the wisdom and perception of people.
- Design-thinking process that underscores the virtue of collaboration to come up with creative solutions (not ideas!).
- Project-based learning in school.
- Algorithms that advise us what to read.
- And now, wall-less classrooms.

Yuval Harari's Homo Deus, and futurists like Ray Kurzweil and Google's Larry Page flesh out the alarming probability and even desirability, of the age of singularity by 2045, where artificial intelligence or super intelligence will supersede human intelligence and will be available for "*one thousand dollars.*"

My stand point is unequivocally clear: nearly all great inventions and discoveries have come from individuals and their team. Teams come into play to turn creative ideas into reality. Moreover, unless we restore the individuality of human beings, and expand their consciousness, we shall not be able to prevent singularity.

Future education must restore the primacy of man over machine.

"Google cannot teach truth, yet."

We are living a post-truth world, a world of alternative facts.

The Big Five – Google, Facebook, Amazon, Apple and Microsoft, dominate our lives and our financial future. They know more about us than we know about ourselves. Their collective market capitalization is worth 3 trillion dollars, making them the largest and most valuable companies on the planet. Their capabilities to influence our thinking, our world view and the choices we make, are more powerful than any state. They have been increasing their ability to manipulate data and information to massage truth and serve their corporate interests. The common man, therefore, faces a dilemma: who is speaking the truth, the Big Five or the state?

The purpose of new learning must be to guard our children and even adults against doctrine, manipulation, post-truth and alternative facts. We are in the midst of an information explosion at unimaginable speed, accompanied by a media blitz on our emotions, and repeated falsehoods to tap into our fears. History is full of examples where a hundred lies can add up to a truth. The challenge for all learners is: how do we know what to believe? Fredrick Nietzsche described the dilemma:

> *"There are two different types of people in this world, those who want to know, and those who want to believe."*

It is natural for human beings to lie for a variety of reasons: lying for fun, covering up mistakes and personal transgressions, for personal advantage, for financial gains, presenting a false image of oneself, or for purposes of deception. Today's social media is narcissistic and is easily manipulated. More often than not, it presents a false reality that makes it increasingly difficult to separate truth from fact. Children lie most often when they are reaching adulthood and when their hormones are in over-drive. Children learn to lie as early as between the ages two and five, reaching a crescendo of 59 percent by the time they graduate from school.

Google's Knowledge-Based Trust has made a beginning by conducting research to develop truth algorithms, that will score millions of web documents and even web sites on their likely correctness and veracity. This will take some time as it is becoming more and more evident that, even Google has its corporate biases, and could create its own reality of the world, of truth.

On balance, because of his or her vast experience and high quality of thinking, it is the great teacher who will be expected to help children and even adults to identify credible information and data. The teacher is the time-tested truth algorithm.

> *"Google cannot give human beings a higher purpose and meaning to life."*

Happiness and self-awareness arise when we give meaning to our lives and our work. They result when we connect what we are doing with a goal larger than ourselves, to a higher purpose. Man continues searching for answers to the existential question: what is the purpose of my life? He has turned to prophets, to gurus, to books. In the *Hitchhiker's Guide to the Galaxy*, author Douglas Adams says that the answer to the ultimate question of life, the universe, and everything, is 42. This is the answer given by the supercomputer Deep Thought after seven and a half million years of processing! In sheer desperation, man has even questioned Google about the purpose of life, Google's latest robot replied, *"To serve the greater good…to live life forever."*

Life, per se has no meaning; we must give meaning to life. Google can't help very much. Each individual has his purpose, his meaning, his vision, his plan. It is very personal and is derived from diverse inspirations: from crucible experiences that are life-altering, from deep reading, deep thinking, and from mentors.

"Google cannot teach life-competencies."

The Fourth Industrial Age has arrived, the age of artificial intelligence, machine-thinking and Homo Deus, where man's aspirations of happiness are becoming possible because of the increasing ability of technology to help us control our inner world.

The revolution in artificial intelligence, machine-thinking and quantum computing is changing the very nature of work. More and more people are searching for work that gives them meaning and not just jobs for money. Traditional methods of formal and structured learning are being replaced by Google content. Moreover, the value of university degrees is declining, and over-emphasis on formal education does not help to prepare students for a life that is volatile, uncertain, complex and ambiguous. With rapid knowledge obsolescence, and present jobs becoming obsolete, the gap between university degrees and future work performance is widening. No surprise, therefore, that world-wide, 53 percent graduates are either unemployed or under-employed.

World business leaders now advocate hiring *"ahead of the curve,"* competencies that exceed present requirements. Skills are on the way out, and only competencies are decisive in hiring. 14 percent Google hirings have never been to college. Ernst and Young, Penguin, Random House and Price Waterhouse Cooper have removed university degrees from their entry criteria, as there is no evidence whatsoever that, university degrees equal success!

Google cannot teach character and values because they are learnt experientially when we connect with communities. Values are learnt by emulating role models at home, great teachers in schools, and developing moral imagination – a sense of what is right and what is wrong. In this regard computers cannot replace human teachers.

> *"Google cannot unlock human potential.*
> *Google cannot create dissonance in order to unlearn."*

Google's AlphaGo can beat the world champion in the Chinese board game GO, and IBN's Deep Blue can beat the world chess champion Garry Kasparov; but artificial intelligence and big data are unable to motivate man and unlock his potential.

Learning has to be preceded by unlearning. Cognitive dissonance is a tool employed by great teachers and leaders through provocation, by questioning and challenging the other's belief system; thus forcing the individual to reconsider his premises built over the years and inherited culturally. Human psychology is such that it either accepts, rejects or modifies one's thinking in order to seek mental equilibrium.

> *"Google cannot help one to achieve excellence in talent."*

Man is born potential and he becomes talent through motivation and deliberate practice. Such form of practice involves mindfulness, getting out of one's comfort zone, setting well-defined challenging goals for improvement, and receiving continuous expert feedback from mentors and great coaches.

The greatest pitfall in talent-growth is having an exclusively knowledge-based approach to learning. In schools and colleges teaching is directed towards *knowing about*. We end up having knowledge but are unable to apply that knowledge in real-life situations. Experience tells us that continuous professional growth is dependent less on attending training courses, workshops, seminars and conferences; and more on developing specific skills, particularly non-cognitive ones. In my experience, the overall gain from such structured training is about 25 percent at best, although many expect it to be as low as 15 percent.

The road to talent is determined more by a skill-based approach; by practising specific skills. Talent development demands a switch from knowing about, to doing. It is not surprising, therefore, that a genius is not a person or scholar having a high IQ, but one who has achieved extraordinary creative results, despite several challenges. Genius is creativity. Therefore, a genius is made, not born. To make someone a genius, Google can do very little.

"Google cannot teach how to welcome and celebrate failure."

To succeed one has to fail first, this being a necessary condition for success. To cope with failure one needs grit; that indomitable spirit displayed by great geniuses like Albert Einstein, the greatest scientist ever known; and Sir John Gurdon, the great English developmental biologist who was awarded the Nobel prize in 2012 for discovering how mature cells can be converted to stem cells.

On 06 June 1907, the University of Berne rejected Einstein's application for a doctorate as a precondition to appointing him as an Associate Professor. They found his thesis more artistic than *"actual physics."*

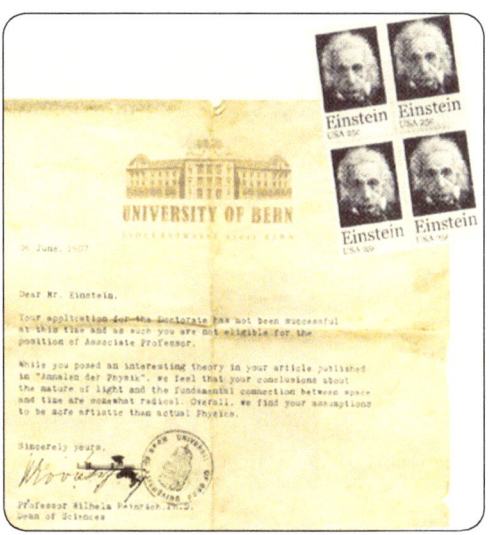

Sir John Gurdon's story is equally mind blowing. When studying at Eton, he was ranked last in the Biology class amongst 250 boys, and was at the bottom of all other Science subjects as well. The headmaster wrote in his school-leaving report, *"I believe he has ideas about becoming a Scientist; on his present showing this is quite ridiculous."* The headmaster could never have imagined even in his wildest dream, that the young lad would one day become the Godfather of cloning.

Einstein, John Gurdon and thousands of other geniuses who experienced failure; they all displayed grit, a combination of extreme passion for something they loved, a driving purpose, that gives meaning, perseverance for long-term goals, positivity and resilience. Google cannot teach this psychological conditioning of the human mind. Leadership, entrepreneurship and scholarship go beyond Google.

The chapters that follow present a strong case in history's greatest tipping point: the struggle between super-technology and human consciousness. Is the jury still out?

I rest my case.

Chapter 1

Purpose and Meaning to Life

Every individual must have a higher purpose – something to live for, something to die for. This is the trinity – purpose, creating meaning in life, and designing a powerful vision to begin the journey of man. Life must have a higher goal, otherwise it makes nonsense of what we believe in, our religion, our God, even in ourselves. The journey is about a higher purpose that gives meaning to life. Without a purpose there can be no meaning, no vision, no happiness.

There is a huge difference between human beings and animals. This is typified in the Sanskrit sloka: आहार – निद्रा – भय – मैथुन. Translated; it means that food, sleep, fear and mating are acts common to animals and humans, and is part of what is described as contentment. The difference lies in चेतना (chetna) or Awareness – awareness of what we are doing, awareness of who we are. Mark Twain once said, *"The two most important days in your life are the day you are born, and the day you find out why."*

Life per se has no meaning; we create meaning to life by pursuing a higher purpose. A purpose has to be transcendental, that is to say, it is larger than the individual, and beyond the confines of one's immediate circle – family, friends and followers of one's faith.

Life per se has no meaning; we create meaning for life.

How do we give meaning to our life? Imagination alone is not enough. We give meaning by connecting our work, our life, to a higher purpose. For example, a teacher teaches the child, and not the subject alone; because her higher purpose is to prepare the child for a future we do not know. Likewise, a stone mason chips away at blocks of stone, not to raise columns to make a cathedral. Rather, he considers himself being part of a team that is making a house of prayer, for followers of the faith to experience divine healing and solace.

In the process of reaching out, we reach inwards, we create meaning. Having a purpose or meaning is not enough – the job is incomplete – we must create meaning for others. For example, true happiness arises only when we make others happy – share our happiness. This is shown schematically.

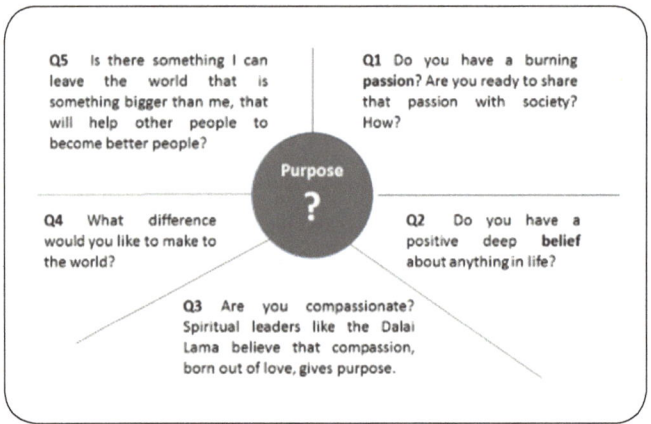

The Purpose of Life - Meaning and Happiness

Meaning enhances one's capacity to deal with suffering, and gives one strength, even in dire situations. The great Viennese psychiatrist, Viktor Frankl once said that, *"suffering ceases to be suffering the moment it finds a meaning."* As a result, it is possible to turn a personal tragedy into a personal triumph.

There has to be a creative purpose for why man exists.

There must be a purpose for human creation, to why we are born, and why we are different from rats or cockroaches. Human beings could not have been created just to be born, to procreate, to feel enjoyment, to work, and to die. There has, therefore, got to be a creative purpose for why man exists. To doubt whether life has meaning is a human characteristic. Animals never raise such questions. They survive and thrive by their instinctive intelligence alone.

A key role for all leaders is to pursue a higher purpose, and help others to do likewise, thus giving meaning to life. Everything we do must have a well-defined purpose – purpose for the self, purpose of business, purpose of education, and a purpose for life. Our vision, our goals, and our roadmaps: they all emerge from the purpose. The purpose is the fountainhead, the source, and the beginning of the journey. The purpose is our location on the GPS map of creation.

The ultimate purpose of life is to be happy. John Lennon recounts his experience with happiness. *"When I was 5 years old, my mother always told me that happiness was the key to life. When I went to school they asked me what I wanted to be when I grew up. I wrote down 'happy.' They told me I didn't understand the assignment, and I told them they didn't understand life."* Irrespective of the varied paths we may choose, happiness is ultimately man's supreme goal.

Most people are fearful of answering the question: '*What is the purpose of my life?*' Change is something most people fear because they fear that it may change their lives completely. To achieve happiness, human beings are motivated by either pleasure, power, or meaning. When there is a feeling of meaninglessness in life, people resort to meaningless acts like crime, drugs, and violence. The will to power and will to pleasure are poor substitutes for will to meaning, because they provide only temporary satisfaction.

Happiness arises when we give meaning to life, to work, to relationships. Meaning arises when man seeks a higher purpose, a higher goal. This is the formula for happiness. Skeptics, however, argue that there is already too much suffering in their lives. To them I say that if life has a meaning, then suffering too must have a meaning. Every person is capable of finding meaning. Although it may sound idealistic, it is possible to promote man to what he should be capable of becoming. The great 18th century German philosopher and playwright, Johann Goethe, was prophetic in his hope for mankind:

> *"If we take man as he is, we make him worse. But if we take man as he should be, we make him capable of becoming what he can be."*

The 2010 Hollywood movie *127 Hours* is the true story of mountain climber Aron Ralston. While trekking in the canyons of Utah, he slips and falls into a crevice, and his right arm is pinned under a boulder. He lies trapped for 127 hours with no food, no water, and no help. In desperation, he amputates his right arm with a Swiss knife, scales a 65 feet high wall, and walks eight miles before being rescued. Aron proved that we can do anything when we choose life. There is no limit to human potential because it is possible for everyone to turn a human tragedy into a personal triumph. Aron exemplified Friedrich Nietzsche's purpose of life: *"He who has a strong enough 'why,' can bear almost any 'how.'"*

- Aron Ralston held on to dear life because he had a reason to live – a vision of his future son.

> *"I was at peace with the idea of me dying. But then I saw this vision of this little boy and it shifted me, it gave me hope to get out because this is my future son."*

Aron survived because of his will to live. With a basic Swiss knife he amputated his arm and freed himself. Each one of us possesses the tools to transform adversity into something positive and shining. We can do it when the time comes.

Those who survived in the concentration camps of Auschwitz and Dachau were not the young or the strong. They were people who had a strong belief in a positive future – something to live for. They were people who believed that life is a gift, that life is beautiful. While man is capable of being evil, he is also capable of doing good. Robert Benigni's Oscar winning Hollywood movie, *Life is Beautiful*, portrays a divine vision of life – that life has meaning even under dire circumstances. The movie sends a clear message: life is a beautiful gift despite its dark side. It is what one makes of it. We always aspire to a life that is ideal, free from pain and worry. A higher purpose enables us to live life as it is.

Suffering has meaning only under the condition that one cannot remove the cause of suffering. What matters most is the attitude one adopts towards a situation that cannot be changed. Viktor Frankl, the renowned Austrian psychiatrist and survivor of the Holocaust, offers sound advice to skeptics:

> *"When we are no longer able to change a situation; we are challenged to change ourselves."*

It is quite irrelevant what the purpose is as long as it is transcendental. That is to say: the purpose should be for someone other than for oneself, or even those who are close and dear. The purpose is something more important than you are, and you are prepared to dedicate your entire life to it. A person who spends 10,000 hours becoming a great pianist is not pursuing a higher purpose. Again, parents who sacrifice everything for their children are not pursuing a higher purpose. They are seeking excellence for themselves, not others.

Purpose should be for someone other than for yourself.

Second, the purpose of living must be ethical and creative, by making a difference in the quality of lives of other people, even people one may not know. Lastly, we must rid ourselves of destructive thoughts and emotions when embarking on the journey to give meaning to life. Overcoming destructive emotions clears the way towards higher emotions like compassion and love. Unless we are conscious of the negative emotions within us – like anger, lust, arrogance, fears, whatever – they will prevent us from achieving our vision and goals. They are distracting and will invariably consume all our positive energies.

The purpose must be ethical and creative.

The Existential Crisis in Man's Life

The 21st century is characterized by volatility, and uncertainty. The acceleration in life is intimidating. It is for the first time we cannot take our foot off the pedal, unable to pause, reflect and reconnect with our selves. It is, therefore, no surprise that, irrespective of one's background, large numbers of people continue to face an existential crisis in their life.

For the first time in our lives we cannot take our foot off the pedal, unable to pause, reflect and reconnect with our selves.

- An identity crisis of who am I? What is my purpose? Where am I going? This human crisis inevitably leads an individual to question whether her/his life has any meaning or value?

- The absence of beliefs that act like a beacon when in troubled waters.

- Facing the grim realities and conditions of life like death, sickness and suffering, retirement from work, especially on becoming senior citizens, financial and career setbacks, and broken relationships.

- Ups and downs in friendship, social disconnect, anxiety about the future, and one's inability to adapt to high-speed change, are leading to loneliness and boredom. Loneliness is assuming such alarming proportions, that the United Kingdom has appointed a minister for loneliness. Even senior citizens are no exceptions. Many are teetering on the brink of depression as they are unable to spend alone-time with themselves. Their lives are an unbroken string of activities.

The symptoms of one's existential crisis are subtle and, therefore, often go unnoticed until it is too late. They can be as innocuous as sleep deprivation, the feeling you don't have enough friends, long hours on Facebook and WhatsApp, craze for shopping, "mall-hopping," and bingeing on food and sensual pleasures. However, there are serious psychological conditions that must be taken note of.

- Declining empathy levels world-wide. Empathy Deficit Disorder, combined with sociopathic behaviour are evident in extraordinary levels of self-focus, addiction to social media and mobile phones, difficulties in personal and family relationships, and low emotional quotient.

- Existential depression and being stressed out by the premise that, life is meaningless. Everything we do, every dream we have, won't be there forever. Under these conditions, self-esteem is the first casualty, as many of us do not consider ourselves as the most important person on the planet.

- Stress and psychological responses like frustration, anger, sadness and anxiety, workplace and life stressors are a global phenomenon, that are eroding happiness levels, employee engagement and productivity. The knock-on effects are concerning:
    - One-third workers claim they are disengaged.
    - Of those who are stressed, two-thirds say that, they are finding it difficult to cope with increased expectations at the required speed.

- There is scant role-clarity in a job which is growing increasingly interdisciplinary and complex.
- Teachers who are expected to prepare children for an uncertain future, are struggling with a stress epidemic and rising mental health issues.

- Declining moral values in the past four decades is a reflection of decline in quality of life, the quality of good governance, and even quality of nations. The lack of gratitude, religious fundamentalism, rampant corruption, nepotism and cronyism in public life, lack of respect for the elderly and comparison towards them, and rise in suicides, divorces and abortions are becoming pervasive. Only a few, the very few can fearlessly say that, improving their moral values is work in progress.
- Reduced personal aspirations or long-term hope – what would they like to be in life; what would they like to give in their life to make a difference; and the absence of long-term goals and aspirations to attain excellence.
- Negativity and pessimism are common. Surprisingly, there is a section of society that believes that there is positive power in negative thinking, and that there are even benefits in being a pessimist. Negative people are toxic because they spread pessimism. To be negative is to see the dark side of life itself and not just problems. Their traits are well demonstrated: they love the word 'but,' they give ten good reasons why a task cannot be done; they are pessimists and they enjoy secrecy.

Strategies to Give Meaning

Gurus show only one path, their path, to give meaning to life. In reality, there are several paths, and often, it will be a mix of permutations and combinations. The key idea to remember is that it is the pursuit of a higher purpose that gives meaning. The strategic options are myriad.

Strategies to Give Meaning

#	Strategy
1	Higher Purpose – Crucible
2	Innovation
3	Beliefs
4	Servant Leadership
5	Living a Value
6	Bucket-list
7	Unlocking Potential
8	Code of Living

Strategy #1: Crucible Experience

The word 'crucible' is a derivative of a vessel used by ancient alchemists to heat various ores to a temperature, where they are transformed into gold. From a leadership perspective, a crucible experience is one that has a deep emotional impact on a person. It is, therefore, life-altering and transformational, as it is founded on the belief that, adversity brings out the best in nations as well as in individuals – through night and blood to light! As a result of the crucible experience, the individual arrives at a new sense of identity, a new vision, a new mission.

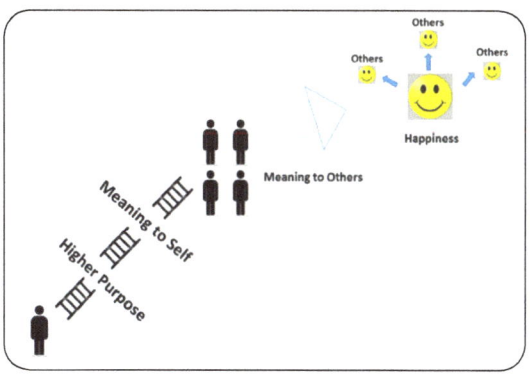

But there is a catch and surprise element: any experience, however powerful it may be, is meaningless unless one reflects upon it. I learnt little from some of the wars and conflicts I had experienced, because I did not reflect on them. It is only much later in my military career, when commanding a Corps in Northern Kashmir that, I consciously reflected and introspected on my crucible experiences. I then realized that life must have a purpose that goes beyond being a General, or being famous or rich.

The crucible is the most effective form of transformational leadership; there is no better substitute for leadership development. The crucible effect could happen in minutes and hours, as Gandhi experienced when he was thrown off a train at Pietermaritzburg, in South Africa, for travelling in first class in 1893. Prince Siddharth (later Gautam Buddha) would visit the interiors of the capital city of his father's kingdom, only to witness the suffering of the old, the sick and the dying. He felt deep compassion for them and decided to give up his kingdom and became an enlightened Buddha. Closer to our time, on 01 December 1955, Rosa Parks who worked as a seamstress in Montgomery, took a seat in the first row of the bus, and refused to give up her seat to a white passenger. This was the spark that ignited the civil rights movement in the United States.

> *The crucible is the most effective form of transformational leadership; there is no better substitute for leadership development.*

Unlike Buddha, Gandhi and Rosa Parks, one does not always have to wait for a crucible event to happen. Leaders and teachers can design crucible experiences having a high-octane fallout. Those undergoing the experience can be inspired to reflect, extract insights, critically examine their values, question their assumptions, and form a belief system.

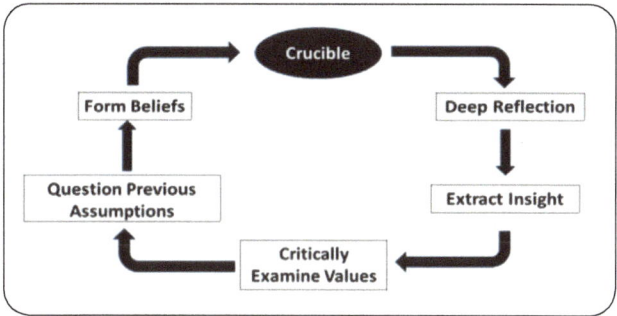

Strategy #2: Innovation

When the purpose of innovation is the common good, to transform the world into a better place and ameliorate suffering, the very act of innovation is transformative; gives life. Innovation may not be only for ideas, products and business models (Air bnb and Netflix); it may even transform professions such as education, or even re-invent an individual. In education, for example, the following would qualify for innovation.

The very act of innovation is transformative; gives life.

- Providing equal opportunity education to the privileged and less-privileged sections of society, thereby making quality education a human right.
- Self-directed learning to personalize learning without the use of technology, as it has been done in Mary Ward School in Toronto.
- Collaborative learning by AI (robots), human teachers and students as learning companions – a fusion of Artificial Intelligence and human intelligence.

Strategy #3: Belief-System

Having and practicing a belief system is the 3rd alternative to a crucible experience. We do what we believe in, and our beliefs are shaped by culture, religion, environment and our experiences. It is, therefore, only natural that beliefs mirror our thoughts and ideas; they are central to who we are. Gandhi is an excellent example. He always said, *"Be the change you wish to see in the world."* When asked to describe Gandhi in one sentence, his biographer, Louis Fischer said that he was one of the rare persons who practiced what he preached.

Beliefs guide our thoughts, our actions, our future, as well as the future of others.

Beliefs guide our thoughts, our actions, our future, as well as the future of others. A belief can be one's purpose in life.

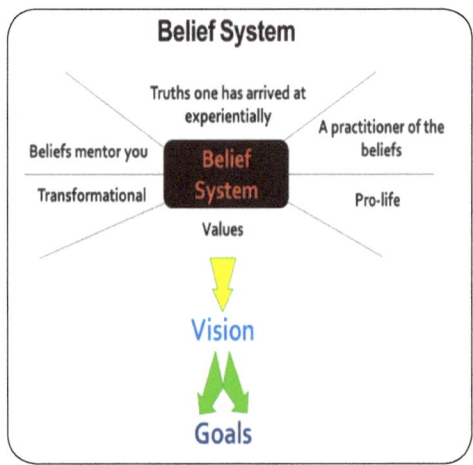

Strategy #4: Servant Leadership

"Servant-leadership" is a term coined by Robert Greenleaf. He defined a leader as a servant first: *"It begins with the natural feeling that one wants to serve, to serve first… Then conscious choice brings one to aspire to lead."* Servant leadership is leadership (often without any title), that replaces one's self-interest by service to others. Instead of employees

serving the leader, the leader serves the employees. A servant leader helps individuals to optimize their full potential and talent – he/she is generally in the business of unlocking their potential.

The servant leaders' bottom-line is clear: to serve the common goal – the community and those he/she is responsible for. Martin Luther King, Jr, epitomized the concept of servant leaders, when he said, *"Life's most persistent and urgent question is, "what are you doing for others?"* Servant leadership could, therefore, be for the common-good, developing the potential of those one leads, or a social/ethical/political cause.

> *"Life's most persistent and urgent question is, "what are you doing for others?"*

In my last military assignment as the Corps Commander of 14 Corps in Ladakh (Kashmir), I was faced with incipient insurgency, which was spilling over from the Kashmir Valley and from across Baltistan in Pakistan-Occupied-Kashmir (POK). My sense of history convinced me that, political power does not come out of the barrel of a gun. I, therefore, decided to win over the alienated communities into the country's mainstream – the common goal, peace in the region.

Servant leaders need great qualities of heart and mind to pursue a higher purpose for others. These are:

1. Compelling vision to transform an organization, homogenize diverse communities, or meet the political and social aspirations of people.
2. Empathy, compassion and forgiveness.
3. The courage to accept mistakes in the past, and the promise to convert them for the community's benefit.
4. Innovative strategies to lead the movement.

5. Grit and resilience to deal with failures and challenges that are unavoidable, and often preordained.

6. The servant leader, must be a persuasive communicator. This attribute is less about having the attributes of a TED speaker; rather it is about winning the trust of the people first. If they trust the messenger, they will trust the message.

7. Leading by example – a role model.

Strategy #5: Living a Master Value

Values are spiritual. When practiced as a way of life, they make one self-aware; they help in knowing one self and give meaning. Leading a life guided by a core value, is a life that subordinates wealth, fame and power. Value is not just an ethical principle or moral, it is what one values most in life, what gives us purpose.

> **Practise Value = Know Yourself**
> **No Value = No Me**

Individuals and organizations can select any value they consider important to guide their life and work. The reader will notice that all great institutions and corporations have a guiding value in their vision statement. It is the repeated practice of the value that, enables an organization to be institutionalized and an individual to become self-aware.

The following steps are recommended for individuals:

- **Step 1:** Select and write down any value you think is most important to you, and why? Then have complete clarity on your understanding of that value. For example, the value of discipline goes well beyond its military understanding. It's more about self-control, moderation and avoidance of instant gratification. Likewise, love is about sacrifice – giving away what is most precious to you for the sake of a person or a cause.

- **Step 2:** Translate the value into three key behaviours for oneself and at one's workplace. These skill-based behaviours should be capable of being taught, observed and measured. An example of three behaviours that support the value of love could be:

    1. *I teach mathematics to X number of children in grade 10 in the local community, at least twice a week.*
    2. *I spend about 90 minutes thrice a week after school hours, to provide pedagogical support to stragglers in my class.*
    3. *I mentor six children in order to unlock their potential.*

- **Step 3:** Seek continuous feedback on how effectively you are living that value. Then reflect and make suitable corrections, if necessary.

Strategy #6: The Bucket List

Popularized by the Hollywood film in 2007, actors Jack Nicholson and Morgan Freeman epitomize the bucket list concept as a set of personal lifetime challenges. This strategy envisages that before one "kicks the bucket" ("to die"), there are a list of things or experiences one must achieve in one's life time. They could be travel and adventure related, or even writing a novel.

A set of personal lifetime challenges.

A bucket list is a collection of dreams, aspirations and goals one would like to achieve in one's lifetime – that inspire you to live, to look forward to. There are several people who have bucket lists, but they are solely for their purpose, their experience. Such lists are limited in scope because they do not give one the desired happiness. True happiness arises when the bucket list experience benefits others also. To be happy is not enough; to make others happy is more important.

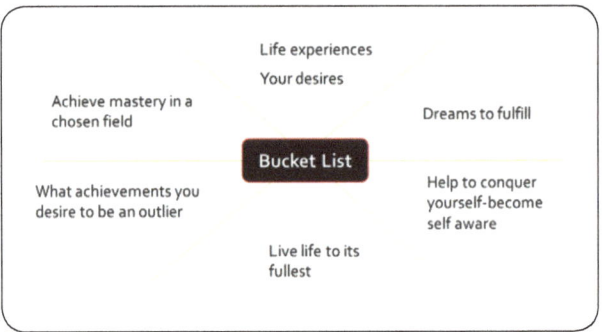

Strategy #7: Code of Living

Happiness is the ultimate human aspiration, and arises through self-awareness, and being able to create meaning in one's life and work. Being happy oneself is not enough; one has to make others happy too. Believers, agnostics and atheists pursue this spiritual objective by seeking a higher purpose; a purpose that is larger than the individual, and is, therefore, transcendental. Put simply, the purpose is to benefit others.

Believers argue that their purpose is practising the fundamentals of their religion. Strictly speaking, this argument is narrow since man does it primarily for himself and his religious flock, and not for humans belonging to other religious and non-religious denominations. However, there are religions like Sikhism, Christianity and Buddhism which are altruistic and require service to all humanity in need, not just those of their own persuasion and beliefs. For that matter so is Hinduism, which regards all created beings as part of the family of man *(Vasudeva Kutumbakam)*.

Irrespective of what route is selected, there is a need to have a platform to pursue a higher purpose. This platform is one's code of living. I believe that the probability of achieving one's higher purpose increases, when/if it is supported by an appropriate credo. The Japanese call it their *Ikigai*, and the Swedes, the Danes and the Finns, describe it as *lagom, hygge,* and *sisu,* respectively.

Although these lifestyles are cultural in nature, they are designed around the following common codes on how to live one's life.

1. **Balanced living,** by avoidance of extremes and practising moderation as a virtue, i.e., *"not too little, not too much, but just enough."* Work-life balance, gender balance, environmental sustainability and fair play, are intrinsic subsets of this concept.

2. There is a big difference between mental fitness and robustness. The former is cognitive, and includes self-efficacy, mindfulness to focus on one's vital few – the 20 percent in Pareto's 80/20 Principle, and exercising self-control. Mental robustness, is a state that goes well beyond mental fitness, and includes emotional intelligence as well as spirituality as under:

   Mindfulness that induces flow.

   Emotional Intelligence.

   Standing up for one's beliefs and ethical principles.

   Setting challenging goals to unlock one's potential.

   Competing against oneself, and not others.

   Having a positive mental attitude.

   Celebrating failure and discomfort as the first step towards success, and being resilient to bounce back into the game.

3. **Aloneness,** by focusing on oneself, to include deep reading, meditation, exercise, and minimum seven hours sleep daily.

4. Being with nature as often as possible, in tune with all creation.

5. Self-reflection underscores our code of living. At the time of his death, Socrates made a profound statement: *"An unexamined life is not worth living."* Socrates' philosophical view of life

claimed that, it is only in striving to know and understanding oneself, do our lives have any value for meaning. The spiritual practice of self-reflection is found in most religions, from the time of Christian desert hermits, to the Japanese samurai, to Naikan in present times. Developed by the Japanese Ishin Yoshimoto, the practice of self-reflection was popularized by Ben Franklin. He wrote down a list of thirteen virtues, and each day he evaluated his day's contribution against one of the virtues.

6. Daily self-reflection is a fundamental aspect in one's code of living. The Naikan practice of *"inside looking,"* should be conducted every day for about 10 minutes. The place selected should be quiet, and the following three questions should be asked:

    1. What have I received from _____?
    2. What have I given to _____?
    3. What troubles and difficulties have I caused _____?

Experiential Approach to Purpose

A significant number of people may find it difficult to follow the various strategies discussed above. The reasons are varied: understanding of seemingly esoteric words like 'purpose,' 'meaning' and 'beliefs,' or challenges in implementation. There is also a mistakenly underlying thought that, in order to seek a higher purpose, a person must withdraw from life and become a hermit.

An easier, practical and experiential approach is an alternative way to seek a higher purpose in one's life. The first approach is to start with children as young as four and five years old. It is easier to start children on the journey of seeking a higher purpose, because they are more spiritual than adults as they have:

Higher levels of empathy and creativity.

A moral imagination, and better sense of right and wrong.

An innocent like understanding of values.

A team sense, because children collaborate more and better than adults.

The experiential journey for a child begins by asking the question: what would you like to do now to heal the world, or improve the quality of life of the local community? The child is then encouraged to set a personal example.

For adults, three practical steps are recommended to happen concurrently.

- First, servant-leadership through community service in the neighbourhood, to make a difference in the local area. Community service is not about raising funds, making websites and designing apps, but about action, about doing. The benefits are immense as it instils:

    Self-pride, self-esteem, and sense of accomplishment.

    Empathy, compassion and creativity.

    Makes the person a good human being.

- Second; design-thinking is a collaborative process to identify problems and solve them creatively. The 5-step process: Empathizing, Defining the problem, Ideating, Prototyping and Testing; helps in developing the competencies of:

    Empathy.

    Creativity.

Critical-thinking.

Collaboration.

- Third; the habit of book reading, followed by a passion for deep reading. Deep reading leads to deep thinking and deep learning. Deep reading is the story of man, the unravelling of the mystery of man: Dostoyevsky's search to solve this mystery exemplified in his writings:

   > *"Man is a mystery. If you spend your entire life trying to puzzle it out, then do not say that you have wasted your time. I occupy myself with this mystery, because I want to be a man."*

The experiential process includes, and is exemplified schematically.

Critical thinking.

Creativity and curiosity.

Assessing indirectly, the experiences of others.

Reflection and introspection.

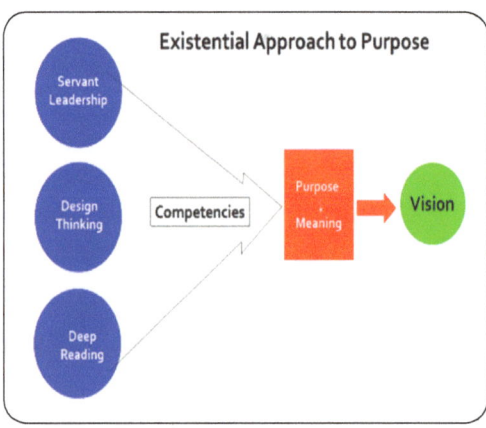

In today's volatile and uncertain world, giving meaning to one's life and work has relevance more than ever before. The need for purpose is a defining necessity in today's world that is experiencing an existential crisis of unmanageable proportions in an increasingly VUCA environment. VUCA times call for purpose and meaning.

Most of the stress and unhappiness in life is because of the absence of meaning. In a culture obsessed with selfishness and pleasure, meaning strikes a spiritual chord towards a richer and a happier life. The journey becomes easy when children are sensitized about why, despite being so young they can heal society.

The search for one's purpose has to start early, as early as in three-year olds. At this tender innocent age they have decisive advantages over adults by way of empathy, creativity, understanding concepts, moral imagination, values and about what is right and wrong.

Chapter 2

Personal Vision

With the advent of the 4ᵗʰ Industrial Age driven by Artificial Intelligence and machine-thinking, we are on the treadmill all the time. There is no time to pause and reconnect with ourselves. The speed of acceleration is awesome and change is the new normal. In such an expanding landscape, everything will change around you and beyond you. But the only constant will be the vision. This is the master strategy for adaptability, for survival, for happiness, for success in a VUCA world.

Leaders begin their journey with vision, irrespective of whether the vision is for the organization, for self-actualization or to make a difference in society. The vision is the start point for excellence, for transformation, for self-actualization, for happiness, for everything.

There is a difference between personal and professional vision. The latter aims at achieving excellence and mastery in one's specific profession. In the process, we are able to lead a life rich in quality. On the other hand, personal vision aims at one's own moral growth and that of others. Accordingly, the professional vision is for Economic Man (for prosperity and productivity); and the personal vision is for Moral Man (a good life based on being good and doing good). Both can co-exist.

The vision is the end state, an imagined future, and the mission is one's determination of how one will get there. The vision is like the heart; it tells you where to go; it is therefore inspirational. The mission is the head; it tells you how to go; it is therefore logical. Of the two, vision is decisively more significant because it is creative, because man's primary duty is to give birth to himself. Goals on the other hand, are more mechanistic, requiring grit and resilience to achieve.

For any transformational leader, a personal vision is imperative. When people do not have a personal vision, they cannot be expected to understand the vision of one's organization; they cannot be expected to reach their full potential. They are hesitant to pursue a personal vision because they do not regard themselves among the most important persons in the world. Without vision, transformation cannot happen. We need to look at leadership not as an exclusively personal achievement, but from the perspective of becoming a whole-person.

Personal vision is for Moral Man.

We live in an unknowable world. With each passing day the world is becoming more and more volatile, uncertain, complex, chaotic and ambiguous. Life, politics, economics, changing jobs, environment and relationships are in a state of constant churning, and no one is sure what the final outcome will be. However, while everything will change, for that is the law of life, the only constant will be man's vision, a vision of his desired future. The personal vision enables a person to empower himself, to take charge of his life and destiny, and unlock his potential to become what he is capable of becoming and being happy in the process.

A personal vision is not about developing one's talent, seeking excellence in one's profession and family, or achieving profits for the organization one serves. A personal vision is a leadership manifesto to give yourself an identity, moral authority, uniqueness and meaning to life. Great leaders strive to be outliers and do not settle for being like everyone else. They are different; even imitating them is difficult, if not impossible. It is potential; it is experiential, an arduous journey through which the hero travels to:

- Seek a higher purpose, in order to achieve to become what Maslow calls self-actualization or self-awareness. The higher purpose could be triggered off by either a crucible experience or a belief.

- Make a difference to society, feeding the hungry, empowering women, educating illiterates, and providing equal opportunities to the under-privileged.
- Leave behind a leadership legacy. A legacy is not what you want to be remembered for, but what you want your people to be after you leave.
- Set challenging goals and raise the bar to reinvent yourself.
- Acquire a personal vision to give yourself an identity, moral authority, uniqueness and meaning to life.

Holistic Growth

A personal leadership vision also enables man's continuous holistic growth, which includes self-renewal in all dimensions – physical, social/emotional, mental and spiritual domain. This happens provided you place yourself centre-stage. The logic is humanistic. I am the most important person in my life. I am the centre of creation. My vision for the development and refinement of myself will invariably bring harmony between work, my family and the community. This is the bottom-line, these are widening concentric circles of growth-self, work, family and community.

Moral Growth

Each one of us can be divided into two opposing personalities: Man 1 and Man 2. Man 1 is economic and represents all the characteristics of the outer world – self-interest, money, power, position, excellence, achievements and sensuality. His legacy is the footsteps he leaves behind on the sands of time.

Man 2 is moral because man does not live by bread alone. He works towards his own moral growth and that of others, of becoming self-aware with the clear objective of being good, making a difference in the lives of those who are underprivileged or in need. The values of love, compassion, respect for life, and Gandhian ideals direct his mission in life. His legacy is not what he wants to be remembered for, but what he wants people and institutions to be and become, when he is no longer there.

A personal vision is set for Man 2; it aims at one's self-growth and that of others. I will not discourage anyone who starts with an economic objective, but later converts it into a moral end. It is, therefore, do-able, for an economic objective to precede a moral goal. It is also possible for Man 1 and Man 2 to co-exist – the outer and inner world living together in harmony.

Man 1 is economic.
Man 2 is moral.

The Vision Process

Step #1: Service, Reflection and Crucible Experience

A humble and most effective way of deciding upon one's vision, is by serving the community even in a modest way; then by gradually increasing the stakes. When one serves people who are marginalized and poor, the heart takes over from the head. The heart will tell you where to go – where your purpose lies. The heart reconnects man with himself.

Get into the habit of deep reflection, using the **"*golden hour*"** in your daily schedule. Reflection and introspection on one's thoughts often helps in finding a purpose. In the words of Socrates, *"The unexamined life is a life not worth living."*

A purpose is often born out of a crucible experience, an experience that is life-altering. Gandhi's crucible experience occurred at the age of 24 when he was thrown out of a first class railway compartment when travelling to Pretoria, South Africa, in 1893. As a result, Gandhi decided to stay back in South Africa for 21 years, to fight social discrimination. That was his purpose. Rosa Park's refusal on 01 December, 1955, to give up her bus seat in Montgomery City gave Martin Luther King, Jr, his purpose – civil rights for black Americans.

Pursuing a purpose does not come without its challenges – how to get the right balance in one's life; how to integrate work, family and the community with oneself; and how to win over stakeholder support.

Step #2: Beliefs Help in Shaping the Vision

The second step is to examine the beliefs we practise. The shaping of one's vision is greatly influenced by beliefs. Beliefs are an individual's world view, as a result of a mixed bag of successes, observations, failures and disappointments. They are also principles and perceived truths shaped by personal experiences and those of others. They begin with self-belief – how one thinks of one self, or self-esteem, one's positive attitude to life, our confidence in our ability to accomplish a task, and clarity in the path leading us along.

A belief is not something that is imposed upon an individual, rather it is what life offers. For better understanding, we must differentiate between knowledge and belief. Knowledge is reason; belief is more of faith than reason. At the end

Beliefs are part of our leadership manifesto.

of the day, it is beliefs that guide our behaviour and actions. Having a belief is not enough, it must be practised day in and day out. Beliefs are part of our individual leadership manifesto.

This leadership vision must echo one's beliefs, and should manifest itself in one's daily life. These beliefs could be social, political, emotional or spiritual. The first step in writing down one's personal vision, therefore, is to put on paper one's beliefs, and then reaffirm whether they are reflected in the leadership vision. As an example, I share below 11 Beliefs that matured in my military and education career spanning over fifty-three years.

1. Man is innately good.
2. Man is born potential. With deliberate effort, practice and feedback, he can become talent.
3. Love is the supreme value because love is God.
4. There is an invisible force that drives the world. While faith acknowledged it long ago, science and reason have yet to accept this explanation.
5. Life, per se, has no meaning; we must give meaning to life by seeking a higher purpose, a purpose that goes beyond one's immediate self.
6. The aim of leadership is to unlock one's human potential first, and then that of others. This is a supreme act of creativity – to give birth to oneself.
7. Success is not winning and losing but about whether one put in all the effort that one could. It's the effort that matters and not winning and losing. For example; the tragedy of life does not lie in not reaching one's goal, but in not having a goal to reach.

8. Great leaders do not derive their power and influence from wealth, position and knowledge, but from moral authority.
9. Greater energy and greater passion is more extraordinary than greater genius.
10. The only perfect person is an imperfect person.
11. Self-actualization is a prerequisite for professional growth.

Step #3: Deciding on the Core Value

The third step in developing a personal leadership vision is zeroing on one's core value. The core value is that value which is most important to you, a value that you hold dear and are prepared to go to any lengths to protect. The core value is the master value that inspires and guides the leader's actions, especially in times of crisis and uncertainty. For Mahatma Gandhi it was *ahimsa* or non-violence. For the Dalai Lama, it is compassion. Your master value is your world view. The master value must resonate in the personal vision statement, as means are more important than the ends.

As a precursor to drafting the vision statement, write down a minimum of three core values that you practise at home and at work. For each, explain your understanding of the value and why it is important to you. Of these, select one master value and provide hard evidence to yourself that you are a practitioner of this value. Try and give a few examples.

The meaning of a given value can be considered at an emotional or a spiritual plane. On an emotional plane, for Man 1, love would be defined as gratitude and caring. But at a spiritual level, for Man 2, love is about compassion and sacrificing what is most precious to a person – wisdom, wealth, time and even life.

Let's take discipline as another example. For Man 1, discipline is more about abiding by rules, punctuality and being a good citizen.

For Man 2, discipline has higher dimensions: self-regulation, mindfulness, delayed gratification, seeking mastery through the 10,000 Hour Rule, and the ability to distinguish between what is right and wrong.

A value that drives the personal vision of Man 2 should decisively be of a higher order.

Step #4: Selecting a Purpose

Finding a purpose in life is the key to one's leadership vision; it is crucial to one's happiness and fulfilment. So how does one set about finding a purpose to give meaning to one's life? We must seek a purpose that goes beyond pleasure and contentment with singular benefits to society as well. The purpose must touch the lives of others and cannot be confined only to one's near and dear ones. A purpose must aim at one's moral growth, and that of others.

Finding a purpose in life is the key to one's leadership vision; it is crucial to one's happiness.

Inside every human being there is a restlessness that arises out of our inability to come to terms with fundamental existential questions such as *Who am I? Why am I here?* Restlessness is a good thing as it is the energy that drives us towards a higher purpose in life. Unless this restlessness is ignited, the journey towards a purpose cannot begin. This is where a mentor plays a critical role in kindling and stoking the fire within the mentee. Besides a mentor, crucible experiences too can bring about this emotional and spiritual transformation.

There are several ways in which we may find a purpose. Gurus and mentors are rare and not easy to find and access, and therefore, one must depend on being a self-mentor. The search must begin with two affirmations:

- I am the most important person in my life. When I change, the world around me also changes.
- I will make a difference in society, however small and insignificant it may be.

Challenges Affecting Our Vision

Challenge #1: How to be the Most Important Person?

There are four key areas of our life that affect the pursuit of a personal leadership vision: work, life, community and self. All four seem to be at cross purposes, raising hackles about work-life balance and time management. While the issue of work-life balance continues to be debated emotively, and will continue to do so ad nauseam, the larger concern is the self.

We spend very little quality time with ourselves, and this is an understatement. There are obvious reasons for this lack of attention. Despite the benefits of Western education, culturally, Asians lack individualism. We are hesitant to promote ourselves in our own eyes. We are also afraid to be alone and talk to our other self. To do so can be painful, often leading to the death of our illusions. We do not seem to grasp the idea that when we spend time improving ourselves, our ability to be better parents, better teachers and better citizens increases exponentially.

Having a personal leadership vision addresses this issue by empowering the individual, which in turn unlocks the hidden potential of those he is responsible to lead and mentor. The key is the self. When that happens, involvement in the community comes about naturally. No other combination can give this result because the gateway to society and community is through an empowered and sensitised self.

Challenge #2: Integrating Self, Work, Family and Community

You can either be the best mother in the world or the best Bharatanatyam dancer, or the best CEO.

In an ideal situation, all the four domains should be integrated, but this is easier said than done. Nevertheless, every attempt should be made as personal and community time can be integrated within one's work and family life. But the exception will happen when one is seeking excellence at work. In such a scenario, you can either be the best mother in the world or the best Bharatanatyam dancer, or the best CEO. This is the price tag, the sacrifice for excellence, and will always be a matter of choice.

Of the available time, can we not spend at least 10 percent of it on our personal leadership journey? This is the spiritual glue that is needed. Is that asking for too much? Anything less would be degrading and belittling one's self-worth. To gain balance in one's life an investment of at least 10 percent of one's time on the self seems very reasonable.

A practical suggested time distribution is given below, and can be varied to suit one's commitments. The impact of personal and community time of 15 percent on work and family life will be phenomenal. With so little, so much is achievable. Is this asking for too much?

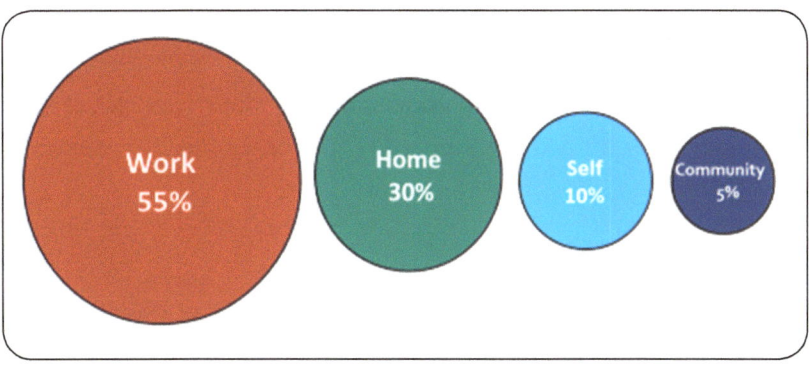

Challenge #3: Stakeholder Support Is Critical

In each of the four areas of life there are stakeholders who have a stake in your future, simply because they are interested in you. Stakeholders are people who exercise the greatest influence upon you. By the same token, you too are able to influence their lives considerably. They exist everywhere, at work, in family, and in the community. However, in your personal domain, you and you alone are the primary stakeholder, unless of course, there is a mentor or a close friend.

As part of the strategy to unlock one's human potential, it is critical that close and intimate support of stakeholders is forthcoming. We must, therefore, identify who these people are, what expectations they have from us, what we expect from them, and how we shall remain in touch with each other. Having identified the stakeholders in each of the four provinces of life, write down what you think their expectations are from you. Then against each expectation, write what you think should be your response, i.e., what they can expect from you. Having understood each other's expectations clearly, you should try and see what compromises are possible, without diluting your vision.

The final stage in stakeholder support will be reached through stakeholder dialogues which could be a mix of formal and informal sessions. These dialogues aim at meeting stakeholder expectations, allaying their fears, and winning their trust and even involvement. These dialogues will help in understanding their expectations with greater clarity, and making them feel special in your self-development.

My Personal Leadership Vision

I share my personal leadership vision as an example of how every leader can join shoulders and minds to unlock the potential of all children.

> I will make a difference to those I am responsible to lead, and the underprivileged, by unlocking their human potential.
>
> I intend to achieve my leadership vision through a combination of personal example, mentoring, providing equal opportunities to the underprivileged, and creating cognitive dissonance.

Irrespective of the vision one sets for oneself, it must lead to one's moral growth as well as those who are affected. A vision that promotes economic growth can't possibly lead to one's moral development. A personal leadership vision, therefore, aims at self-actualization.

The primary reason why most people do not appreciate the power of personal vision is because they do not consider themselves the most important person in the world, and secondly, because their minds are unruly and undisciplined for they cannot focus on essentials and be mindful. The vision ensures our evolution and moral growth and is shown schematically:

Focus Stay Still or Calm

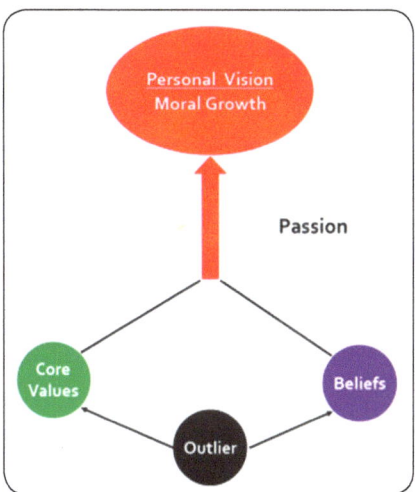

Chapter 3
Unlocking Human Potential

The single biggest crisis in the world is not oil, religious radicalization, the weakening of globalization, corruption, mis-governance, or climate collapse. It is the failure of education, an education system that is not designed to unlock human potential. And the failure of education is the failure of leadership development.

The tragedy of life in most human beings is that they are unable to reach their full potential. And, therefore, their capacity to give back to society is also limited. The primary role of a leader and an education system is to unlock potential – one's own potential, and that of others. In its higher reaches, leadership is about mentoring to unlock potential.

There is a huge difference between *training* and *development.* Leadership training aims at improving business and work performance by refining and mastering strategy, tactics, skills, drills, procedures, techniques, and systems and processes; and is top-down. Leadership training is essentially about governance, management, occupying leadership positions, and the capacity to influence people to one's way of thinking. Leadership development, on the other hand, is about discovering one's potential about self-actualization, leading to happiness – the ultimate human aspiration. This is self-driven. This is leadership.

In my experience, self-development is a prerequisite for professional development. This is explained below schematically.

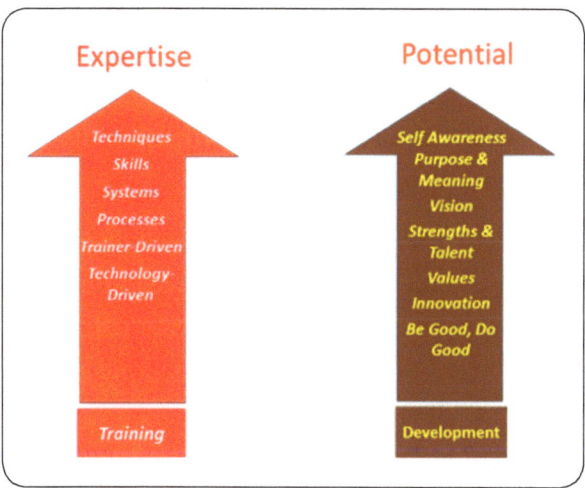

What is Leadership?

In 2015, there were 57,136 books in the Amazon library, with the word 'leadership' in the book title. As if this is not enough, leadership books are being published at the rate of more than four per day or 1460 per year. That makes it over 60,000 by the end of 2017. Over 90 percent leadership books are written by non-practitioners, management consultants, academics, respected journalists, business executives, and even pastors and rabbis. Napoleon Hill was a journalist, so is Malcolm Gladwell. Daniel Pink was a speech writer for Al Gore and is currently a successful author. The overwhelming majority of these writers define leadership as the ability to influence in Dale Carnegie style – *How to Win Friends and Influence People.* John Maxwell, the famous American motivational speaker says, *"Leadership is influence."* In essence, leadership is perceived by non-practitioners as gaining expertise in influencing outcomes, decisions and behaviour.

The unlocking of human potential is complicated by the staggering number of leadership definitions. If the reader googles the word leadership, there are over 4,80,000,000 results! In 2015 alone the global spending on leadership training costs was $ 356 billion. Despite such heavy investments in training, there has been no significant qualitative improvement in either business outcomes or leadership quality to cope with the challenges of the 21st century. Undeniably, companies around the world have not been able to take advantage of rising business opportunities because they lack the right quality of leaders.

In my view, leadership is the ability to lead oneself first; and then others. One must, therefore, set a vision to lead oneself, hold values, pursue a higher purpose and unlock one's potential. *"Leading me is the greatest challenge,"* because, to lead effectively one has to utilize one's maximum potential. In real terms, leadership is transformational, and may be defined as the ability to unlock one's potential and that of one's team; and then focusing all the energy towards achieving a common goal. The unlocking process is an act of innovation as it gives rebirth to oneself.

Leadership is transformational, and may be defined as the ability to unlock one's potential and that of one's team.

Experiential knowledge and scientific experiments bear evidence that at best we use only 8 to 10 percent of our potential. The rest lies submerged like the proverbial iceberg. The leadership challenge, therefore, is how to tap, how to discover, and take full advantage of this potential.

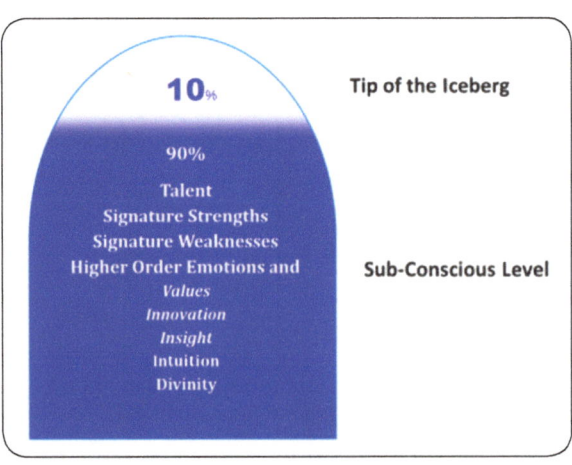

Key Strategies to Unlock Potential

India has a poor track record in creating champions, be they in the field of science, music, sports, innovation and even in schools. We readily accept mediocrity, and are reluctant to push people beyond the envelope, and become unpopular in the process.

Unlocking human potential inevitably leads to transformation – a new identity, a new vision, a new mission. For example, it is not enough to know what my potential is. What is important is to convert that potential into talent and transform myself?

Beliefs in Human Potential

The journey to unlock human potential begins with beliefs that are scientifically proven, and universally acknowledged. They are sacrosanct and are as under:

1. Man is born potential, he becomes talent.
2. Human potential is not fixed as man has evolved from a water molecule to what he is today, and what he will be tomorrow.
3. To realize your potential, you have to fall in love with yourself, because you are the most important person in your life.
4. Man's mission lies in reinventing himself by giving rebirth to himself. He cannot achieve this innovation without help from others.
5. Focus on your signature strengths, your potential; and not on the weaknesses unless they are debilitating.
6. Traditionally, experience is counted by the number of years one has served a profession. Thus, a teacher with ten years of teaching experience is expected to be better and more effective than one with just two years. Research debunks

this belief. Once a person reaches an "acceptable" level of expertise and automaticity or habit, additional years (even with some practice) do not necessarily improve performance. Moreover, *"these automated abilities gradually deteriorate in the absence of deliberate efforts to improve"* (Anders Ericsson, Peak, 2016).

7. Training should focus more on doing (75%) than on knowing (25%). From the viewpoint of deliberate practice, attending courses, workshops, etc, do not offer feedback, the opportunity to learn from mistakes, developing a new skill, role-play, problem-finding, and hands-on experience.

Everything is possible if we believe it is possible. In an experiment, a scientist placed a number of fleas in a jar with a lid on top. The fleas began jumping and hitting the lid. After some time, they began jumping high enough not to hit the lid and thus injure themselves. The scientist then removed the lid as the fleas no longer jumped out of the jar. The fleas had been conditioned to believe that they could not escape from the jar. Unfortunately, most of us are limited in believing that most things are beyond our reach. But, whatever the mind of a man can conceive, can happen. How else would mankind have progressed, in every sense of this word?

With the right motivation and professional mentoring, every man can be what he should be. This deep belief inspires and encourages people to realize their potential. The great German philosopher, Johann Wolfgang von Goethe, has inspired several generations to discover themselves by his prophetic understanding of human nature:

"Treat man as he appears to be, and you make him worse. But treat a man as if he were what he potentially could be, and you make him what he should be."

> *"Treat man as he appears to be, and you make him worse.*
>
> *But treat a man as if he were what he potentially could be, and you make him what he should be."*

This is the manifesto of great leaders and realized mentors.

Seeking a Higher Purpose

On taking over command of 14 Corps in Ladakh in June 2000, I was faced with incipient insurgency spilling over from the Kashmir Valley and Baltistan. We had been to war with Pakistan four times with no conflict resolution; and therefore, a military response was not the answer. I decided to win over the alienated communities – their hearts and minds. I achieved this in just less than nine months through Operation *Sadbhavana,* a mass socio-political campaign. To the credit of the people, nearly twenty years down the line not a shot has been fired, and Ladakh continues to be a zone of peace.

Sadbhavna was a crucible experience for me. A crucible is a life-altering and transformational experience like the one Gandhi experienced when he was thrown out of a first class railway compartment in South Africa, as non-white people were not permitted, or expected to sit where white South Africans did. The word crucible is closely associated with the pseudo-religious science of alchemy. Alchemists used crucibles to purify base metals into gold. I realized, although late in life that, life must have a higher purpose to give meaning to life, to work, to build relationships, and to unlock human potential. It cannot be to become a General, or be rich and famous. That explains why I retired prematurely from the military, to start a family of the best international schools in India.

Challenging Goals

Only challenging goals can unlock potential and transform an individual. By their very nature, challenging goals are goals presently beyond one's capabilities. Challenging goals have a probability of failure as high as 50 percent; they stretch human capabilities to their extreme, are well beyond one's usual comfort zone, and place heavy demands on sacrifice. Only challenging goals drive one forward. Failure must never deter one from pursuing a challenging goal, because failure is good, failure should be welcomed, and failure is the first step to success. People need to be constantly reminded that, even if one fails to achieve the desired goal, what we become as a result of trying to reach the goal is more important. Under these conditions, the journey itself becomes the goal.

Conquering Mount Everest, or completing a series of ultramarathon races in the deserts, Desert Runners, are examples of challenging goals, as they push the limits of their minds and bodies. Reaching out beyond your grasp is what heaven is all about. When this happens ordinary people achieve the extraordinary.

Deep Reading

Deep reading involves careful selection of appropriate books and online text, rapid surface skimming to identify ideas and concepts, followed by mindful reading and understanding of each idea and concept. The very process of deep reading, often involves a mix of digital and text reading, and watching YouTube. The next step for the reader is to identify concepts relevant to his or her organization. Consequently, deep reading triggers off deep thinking, the search for truth, and transports the reader beyond the intellectual world into a spiritual world. In turn, it facilitates unlocking human potential by:

Finding a higher purpose.

Innovation.

Understanding the mysteries of life, such as; is there life after death?

Do people live on other planets?

Seeking inspiration to seek challenging goals.

Questioning dogma, and giving a different perspective on life and issues.

Discover and Nurture One's Signature Strengths

The film *Blindside* is the story about an African-American teenager with a low IQ, poor academic grades, but a massive 98 percent in protective instincts on an aptitude test. His protective instincts go beyond protecting his adoptive sister and brother; and is played out on the soccer field with the teenager protecting the quarterbacks. This leads to stardom in becoming one of the greatest football players in the country. A signature strength is a unique capability which an individual possesses, and is what others think one possesses. A mentor identifies the signature strength of the mentee and leverages that to full advantage.

As leaders, it is critical to identify and focus on the signature strengths of individuals, and then maximize the advantages to unlock their potential.

Tough Love

In the Thesaurus of excellence there are no phrases like *"Well done,"* *"Good job,"* and *"That's awesome."* These are synonyms for ordinariness, for mediocrity. When seeking excellence to unlock potential, leaders and trainers must push the performer to the extreme to bring out his best potential without regard for his feelings. This is called tough love and is brilliantly featured in the film *Whiplash*. The phrase "tough love" first originated in Bill Milliken's book of the same title. He summed up the meaning of tough love as, *"I don't care how this makes you feel toward me. You may hate my guts, but I love you, and I am doing this because I love you."*

> *"I don't care how this makes you feel toward me. You may hate my guts, but I love you, and I am doing this because I love you."*

Tough love is also a thermometer to gauge the learner's grit and passion, in how determined she or he is to uncover her hidden potential.

Tough love is a technique of coaching and mentoring that is demanding and brutal at times, and often necessary to drive home lessons and new learning in the shortest possible time, without compromising quality, by pushing beyond the boundaries of reason and sensibility, and learning through failure.

Deliberate Practice

The proverb, Practice makes perfect, is a myth. Solving a 100 sums, dancing two hours at a stretch, driving a car every day, operating eight hours in a hospital, or having fifteen years of teaching experience in school, does not enhance peak performance. In reality, performance drops! A teacher with two years of experience, but under expert coaching and deliberate practice, is more talented. Practice or effort without professional feedback does not develop talent. In schools, deliberate practice is done through what is called assessment for learning as opposed to assessment of learning. In the former, the teacher advises the student on what improvement is needed, how it is to be done, how it will be measured, and from what source help is available.

Deliberate practice comprises three key components:

1. Talent alone is not enough. The trainee must be intrinsically motivated to improve herself, as deliberate practice is mentally demanding. She cannot be forced into expert performance as this requires high motivation to sustain hard training.
2. The coach lays down measurable physical, cognitive and mental goals and a regimen for improvement, such as change in lifestyle, breaking down goals into specific skills, and setting-up a practice plan.
3. The coach provides immediate feedback on the trainee's performance, and whatever corrective actions are required. Without feedback and reflection, there can be no improvement, and mere practice alone is of no help.

Creating a Hypothetical Model of Excellence

Mentoring is undoubtedly a popular model for unlocking human potential. This is based on the premise that, being in the company of great masters, their mastery rubs off on the learner. This works quite effectively in the context of specific disciplines such as dance, music, golf etc. But not as a leader. We need to adopt an alternative model, if we expect our mentees to be world champions – next generation leaders. The alternative is to build a hypothetical prototype for excellence as under:

- Take any specific craft, a leader, an athlete, or teacher, or whatever, and break it down into designated spiritual, cognitive and emotional skills.
- For each skill search for multidisciplinary excellence. For example, an athlete must be able to perform under extreme pressure. We could select the American Navy SEALs as the designated performance model. The hypothetical model is built around various diverse parameters, such as:

    Spirituality.

    Life skills.

    Psychology.

    Lifestyle.

    Technology.

    Nutrition.

    Health.

- Then benchmark the player against the standards laid down in the hypothetical model for world class performance.
- Create a hypothetical model wherein benchmarks for high performance have been set.
- On completing a SWOT analysis, compare high performers with the global benchmarks identified, and determine where do they stand?

- Set targets for individuals.
- Prepare a training plan.
- Measure performance.
- Improve skills by:

    Practice.

    Feedback.

    Repetition.

    Progression – moving the bar up gradually.

    Creating failure for mental toughening.

Psyche for Unlocking Potential

Unlocking potential places heavy demands on a leader's motivation, energy and commitment. By its very nature, mentoring is transformational. The big question every mentor must ask: Has unlocking the potential of the other person transformed me in any way? In specifics, the demands on the leader are exacting:

1. Strive for excellence: evaluations such as *"Well done & Good Job"* lead to mediocrity.
2. Be prepared for unpopularity in trying to push your team beyond all frontiers.
3. 50% of your time will be invested in unlocking potential.
4. Are you innovative?
5. Unlocking potential must lead to transformation – yours too!

Likewise, mentees must realize that there is a price tag for excellence:

1. Intrinsic motivation and seriousness of purpose.
2. Ready to push all boundaries.
3. Sacrifice what is precious in your life or what is distracting.
4. Disrupt work-life balance if push comes to shove.
5. Mindfulness.

"If you haven't found something you are willing to die for, you aren't fit to live."

– Master Luther King Jr

Unlocking human potential is a deliberate, carefully executed process, and responds to processes and practice which can be studied and embraced by teachers and leaders alike. However, it is always about individuals and persons and their unique traits and methods of learning. Teachers in themselves who have been beneficiaries of such leadership must reflect and plan this drawing out of potential very carefully and deliberately. This sort of leadership requires a subtle but sharp blend of what is professional, and that which is personal, to bring out the best that is in their students and in themselves.

The emphasis in school education has to shift from over-emphasis on training to education. The former is about content, pedagogy and disposition – essential for earning a livelihood. The latter is critical to prepare one for life.

Schools continue to focus on education of the outer-world, the world of nature, resources, people and money. This is already changing rapidly in the 4th Industrial Age. The focus is now shifting to education of the inner world – the education of the heart and mind, and not head alone. This tectonic shift will help unlock human potential.

Chapter 4

Lifelong Learning

The 4th Industrial Age has arrived. Driven by Artificial Intelligence and bio-technology, the changes in the next 15 years will be more numerous and greater than those we have experienced in the past one thousand years. Such is the awesome rate of change and acceleration affecting our life and work. In order to be a lifelong learner, we must learn how to manage change, and accept that change is the normal. It is this adaptive capability that has enabled the human species to evolve. Human beings will stop evolving when they cannot adapt to change.

The contours of this revolution are clearly visible, and we must brace ourselves to adapt before it is too late.

1. Artificial intelligence and automation will dominate every aspect of our life, our work, our bio-chemicals, our genes, our attitudes and even our beliefs.
2. About 40 percent of today's jobs are likely to disappear by 2030. Another 40 percent will undergo change to receive a completely new look, with changes in roles, responsibilities and expectations. For example, we are already witnessing the diminishing role of mechanical engineers as the evergreen branch of engineering. Software engineers are predominantly building drones, robots, electric and driverless cars. And with the introduction

40 percent of today's jobs are likely to disappear by 2030.

of robot-teachers in classrooms, human teachers will be required to re-role themselves as learning companions.

3. Jobs, knowledge and technology obsolescence is changing the landscape of everything, placing heavy demands on individuals to reskill themselves continuously. Those who cannot unlearn and relearn will be illiterates – illiterates who have no political and economic value, and are, therefore, unemployable.

4. Most significantly, formal and structured education is losing its earlier pristine importance. First, the need for continuous reskilling arises because of obsolescence; and second, the increasing importance of "doing," the application of knowledge – Knowledge "to do" and not "knowledge about." Learning is doing, and doing is creating. People are no longer interested in your achievements. They want to know what you have done with those qualifications and experiences.

Formal and structured education is losing its earlier pristine importance.

Clearly, the 4th Revolution has three implications for lifelong learning:

- **First**, lifelong learning and re-skilling will be the mother-of-all competencies for one to survive and be happy. Those who lack this competency will not be employable. And even those who inherit family fortunes and businesses, will find it challenging to hold on to their wealth.

    Lifelong learning and re-skilling will be the mother-of-all competencies.

- **Second**, schools presently prepare students to pass examinations and do not prepare them for life. In order to do so, how to learn should become the #1 pedagogy in schools. This switch places heavy demands on adapting to a new learning culture.

    Students are expected to be their own teachers, and teachers must become their own students.

As lifelong learners, students are expected to be their own teachers, and teachers must become their own students.

- **Third**, the 4th Revolution presents great opportunities – to access our hearts and minds – to know ourselves – to become self-aware – to be happy. In a spiritual sense, lifelong learning is learning about oneself, about self-actualization.

Doctrine of Learnability

To be learnable is to possess an insatiable desire to learn, and acquire new competencies and skills and to innovate. In a philosophical sense, the zest for learning arises only when there is a deep-seated longing to understand the mysteries of life.

The zest for learning arises only when there is a deep-seated longing to understand the mysteries of life.

> *"Man is a mystery, and if you spend your entire life trying to puzzle it out, then do not say you have wasted your time. I occupy myself with this mystery because I want to be a man."*
>
> *– Fyodor Dostoevsky*

One cannot be a lifelong learner if one is not learnable. The key to learning is the ability to learn, unlearn and relearn. Way back in 1970, the futurist Alvin Toffler wrote in Future Shock:

> *"The illiterate of the twenty-first century will not be those who cannot read and write, but those who cannot learn, unlearn and relearn."*

If this principle or yardstick is applied in real earnest, most people would be labelled illiterates even today. Learnability involves knowing how to learn in the first place. Without this competency, personalization of learning and self-directed learning cannot ever happen. Moreover, learning is about doing, about application, and about possessing competencies to apply knowledge, to innovate.

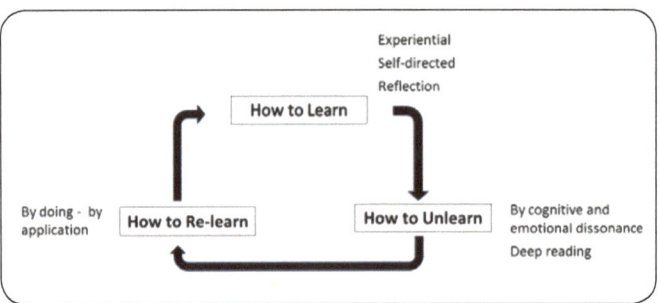

The most challenging attribute of learnability is acquiring competencies for creative solutions to implement ideas and solve problems. We may consider them as part of capacity-building for learnability, implement to include:

The most challenging attribute of learnability is acquiring competencies.

Empathy.

Technology-mindedness.

The practice of deep reading.

Reflection and introspection.

Being concept and goal-minded.

An honest competency-gap analysis will help one to identify specific competencies one is short of. Thereafter, developing them to acceptable levels will be a long haul.

The next attribute of learnability is to be able to learn on the fly, on the job. In order to do so, the learner must acquire the habit of reflection-in-action, i.e., processing information while the event is happening, and drawing upon new insights. Such capabilities enable one in:

- Decision-making, by being sensitive to the environment, and being able to intuitively recognize patterns, and define the problem. Solving it thereafter is relatively easy.
- Making corrections while working and by learning from failures even as they happen, and seizing new opportunities.

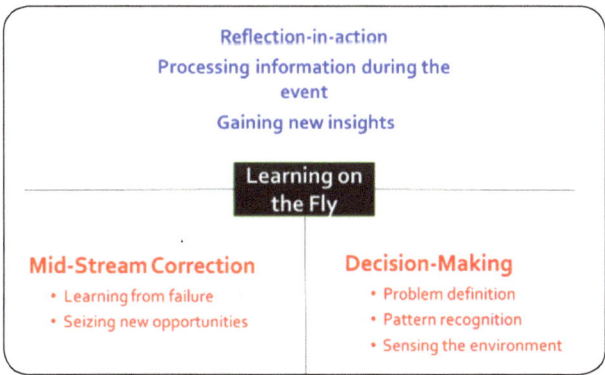

On-the-job learning is the most practical form of learning provided it is done correctly. The concept and application of the 70:20:10 learning model is realistic and exemplary, and is shown schematically.

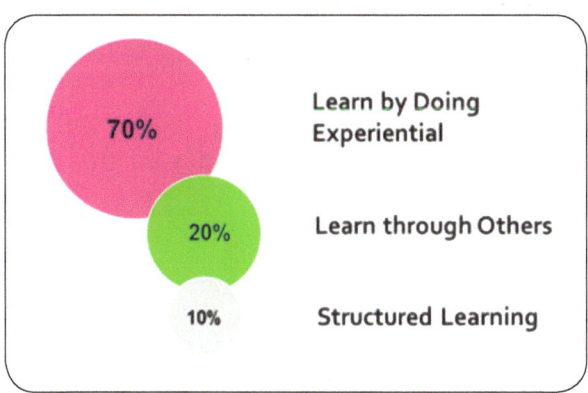

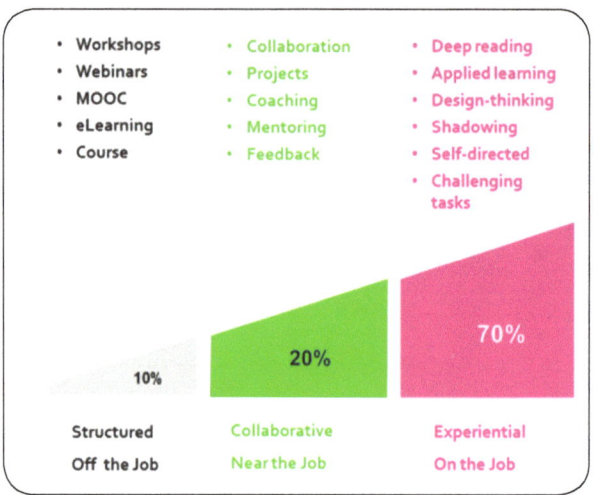

I wish to show my learnability model as an example because it exemplifies the application of the combined capabilities of head, heart and mind. True learning is endurable as it is driven by intrinsic motivation to unlock one's potential.

Learning must be inspired and the inspiration arises from will to meaning – meaning to life and work. It is meaning that motivates a person to unlock one's potential and become self-aware in the process. Meaning, followed by deep reading and technology-mindedness (not necessarily being technology-savvy), provides the foundation for learnability. While there will common methods and techniques of self-learning, each individual must develop her/his own personalized model that suits one's cultural background, strengths and weaknesses. My models are shown as examples.

Learning must be inspired and the inspiration arises from will to meaning – meaning to life and work.

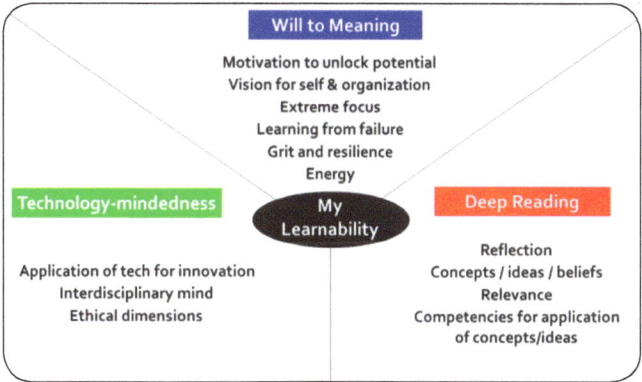

Having developed one's capacity for lifelong learning; and formed a firm foundation; I am ready to learn. A checklist of my learning process is shown schematically:

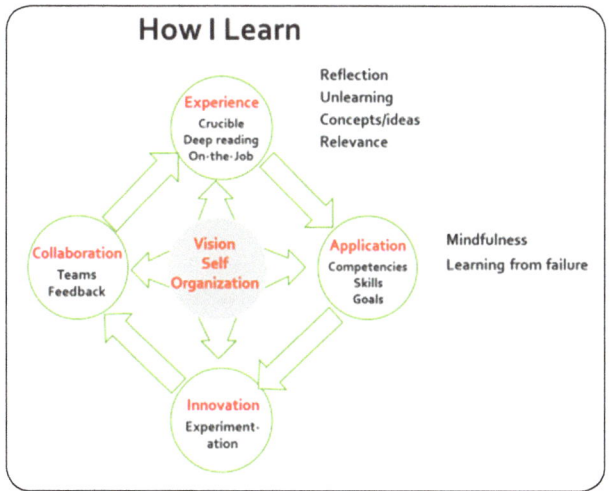

Just-in-time Learning

Today's employee has less than 1 percent time in a working week to dedicate to learning. Just-in-time learning is founded on the premise that every individual is responsible for her training and self-development, because every student is her own teacher. This form of learning is based on the fine-tuned ability to access knowledge, and train oneself to learn anytime, anywhere 24 × 7. One does not have to wait for a specific time and a budget to start training because training is happening all the time.

One does not have to wait for a specific time and a budget to start training because training is happening all the time.

To help this idea, a teacher or a corporate employee always carries a Kindle or a book in her backpack. Whenever an opportunity arises – travelling, commuting, waiting for an appointment, or having idle time, one can read, annotate the text and reflect.

The just-in-time methodology is as under:

- Mobile learning is the most responsive, user-friendly, low-cost, and handy learning device, as more often than not laptops will not be accessible. Mobile phones can access voice, video and text anywhere, and even send answer scripts. The educational benefits of mobile learning are immense both in teaching and learning. Regrettably, schools and even corporations, have yet to exploit its full potential in a meaningful way. Teachers must train and condition students not to use them incessantly as a means of distraction, e.g., always checking messages and mails.

  Mobile learning is the most responsive, user-friendly, low-cost, and handy ever present learning device.

- As the individual is responsible for her learning, she must decide on the best checklists for just-in-time learning. These are:

    Determine competency-gap analysis.

    Establish learning needs and learning objectives.

    Gather essential data.

- Setting learning goals that are supported by detailed plans.

- Create learning networks for collaboration.

- Break down learning requirement into smaller chunks or pieces of information. This enables learning at an early speed.

- Select appropriate training courses like MOOC, Linkedin and social media.

- Read blogs of reputed thought leaders.

- Create a micro learning resource library organized by category and task.

A Learning Culture

In a VUCA world, no one can ever envision when personal disaster can strike. Bereft of entrepreneurial competencies, there is the inevitable danger of not being meaningfully employed. It is, therefore, imperative that we invest time, money and resources in acquiring and practicing these competencies in order to re-skill ourselves continuously.

Of the several implications of lifelong learning for leaders and teachers, five features stand out:

- **One**: Learning is experiential – we learn from crucibles, deep reading, and while on the job.
- **Two**: Learning is by doing, by application of ideas and concepts. Mindfulness, learning from failures and goal-setting are essential tools.
- **Three**: Application must eventually lead to experimentation and innovation.

- **Four**: Acquiring a new Lingua Franca by teachers to comprise:

  Basic coding and AI programming.

  Designing content for AI teaching.

  Design-thinking.

  Deep reading.

- **Five**: It is only through practicing the learning culture that assured mastery is possible. This is a critical factor because innovation, more often than not, happens in one's domain of mastery.

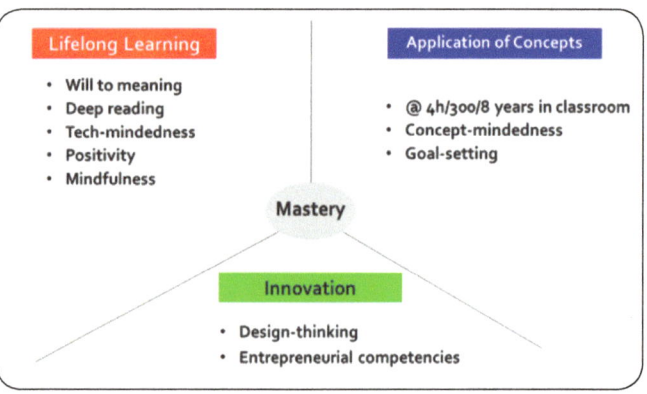

Having acquired working-proficiency in these five features, we as individuals and organizations are ready to shift from a training to a learning culture. The difference between the two are stark.

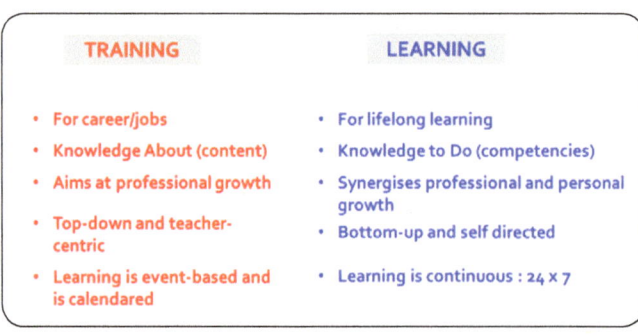

For those accustomed to a training culture, shifting to a learning culture can be challenging. It is undemanding if the culture is introduced at the school level. The key strategies @ school will be:

1. Motivation to learn which emanates from an individual's will to meaning. This is the most difficult part, but could also be the easiest. Unless students are intrinsically motivated to take on the responsibility of their learning, to become their own teachers, the learning culture will remain a pipe-dream.

2. The motivation may be there; but that is not enough. Students should be proficient in the process of how to learn through self-directed learning. How to learn is the #1 pedagogical strategy for school, for work, for life.

3. The most effective form of learning and achieving mastery is by doing, by application of concepts, to find creative solutions to problems. The curricula of schools the world over, are still content-driven. Unless teachers help students to develop competencies – education of the head, heart and mind – learning by doing will remain a distant mirage.

4. Teachers and students should focus on extracting concepts, and understand the relevance of why they are learning what they are learning. A special effort in this direction is required, because text books in school teach children how to pass examinations; and not to understand and apply concepts. In my view, concept understanding is best understood by deep reading, followed up by reflection.

5. Harnessing the power of collaborative learning, through either the design-thinking process, or project-based learning, as they help students in understanding and simplifying complex and inter-disciplinary problems, and coming up with creative solutions.

Collaborative Learning in the AI Age

Future learning is collaborative because knowledge is interdisciplinary, and no single person has all the answers to complex problems. In this model, students, teachers, and AI are equal partners, and for the first time we shall see students being active learners, and teachers personalization of learning by meeting individual student's learning needs.

Future learning is collaborative.

Collaborative learning in a complex world assumes supreme importance because talent no longer resides in individuals. Talent lies in the team. With the arrival of Artificial Intelligence and machine-thinking, students, teachers and AI (robots) will become each other's learning companions. Today nearly 90 percent of a teacher's time is taken up in preparation and delivery of content, assessments and special assignments on campus. This leaves little or no time for the teacher to teach the child, and not the subject alone. Artificial intelligence will take over these tasks and personalization a reality, and make teachers relevant. They will do what they are supposed to – teach the child and not the subject alone by accessing the student's inner world.

Artificial intelligence will take over most of the traditional responsibilities of a teacher, make personalization a reality and empower the teacher. Teachers will now do what they are expected to do – teach the child and not just the subject, and in the process, unlock the child's potential. This is explained schematically:

Teachers will now do what they are expected to do – teach the child and not the subject alone.

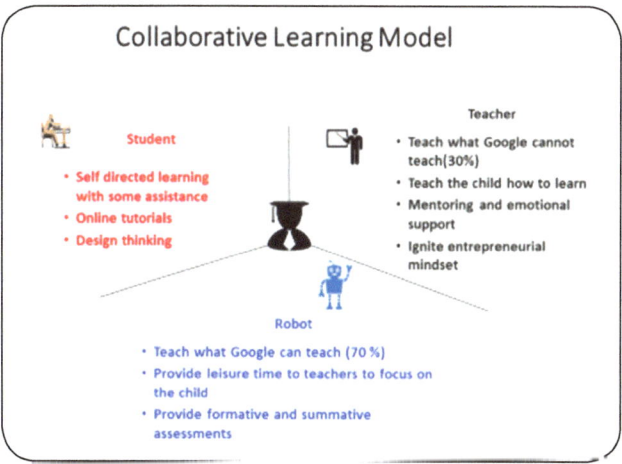

Lifelong learning is not restricted to being successful in one's profession. In a larger sense, lifelong learning is learning about one self – one's self-awareness, one's identity, one's purpose in life, one's aspirations and emotion, one's good and bad. This is an evolutionary process and will continue unabated till one dies.

Lifelong learning, therefore, demands a complete change in lifestyle, and placing the individual centre-stage in the belief that she is the most important person on the planet. A new scaffolding for learning is overdue – the unadulterated commitment that every individual is responsible for her learning. The days of gurus might be over.

Chapter 5

The Renaissance in Innovation

In the 4th Industrial Age, innovation will be the # 1 leadership and spiritual competency. If you are not creative you are illiterate, having no economic and political value. You are a liability to society. From time immemorial, the nature of innovation has been traditional, and has ranged from inventions; to giving the world transformational ideas like democracy and Marxism; creating new products like driver-less cars; new business models like Uber and Airbnb; social innovation like the Grameen Bank, a bank for the poor and solving problems creatively. Now in the 4th Revolution, innovation is taking a quantum leap from the outer to the inner world: to reinvent and reskill oneself continuously, develop an entrepreneurial mindset that will benefit profit, people and the planet; and become Homo Deus.

Innovation will be necessary for economic prosperity, coping with VUCA conditions, sustainability of the planet, self-actualisation and institutional legacy. From 1955 to 2017, only 60 of the original 500 Fortune companies are surviving. The survival rate is 12 percent. It is believed that, in the next ten years, about 40 percent of today's Fortune companies will disappear. The reasons are obvious: no purpose, no vision, and no innovation.

The renaissance for innovation must begin in schools. Schools of the future are schools of innovation. Regrettably, it is schools that continue to kill creativity. If schools resist innovation, Artificial Intelligence will replace teachers with algorithms. This is my prophecy.

Twenty first century school leaders must be at the vanguard of leading the renaissance in innovation.

The Challenges We Face Volatility, Uncertainty, Complexity and Ambiguity (VUCA)

The traditional approaches to leadership need serious review, as they were more suited for what was a stable and predictable environment, where outcomes were well-defined. In such linear situations, it was possible to work out specific goals, detailed plans, and predictable outcomes. Not anymore.

Unlike communication in a stable world that places heavily reliance on persuasion and influence – more on the lines of TED talk formats, communication in a VUCA world will be more on the intent of the higher leader, and the 'why' of a mission. The new process is shown schematically.

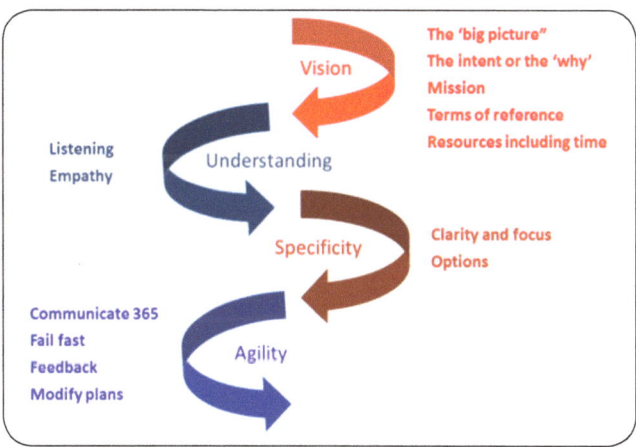

The pace of change is constant and often erratic, and many find increasing acceleration impossible to adapt with. To make matters worse, we are deluged with an information overload of cataclysmic proportions that often leads to anxiety and despair. As if these are not enough, volatility, uncertainty, complexity of problems and ambiguity (VUCA) are taking a heavy toll on problem-solving, decision-making and designing strategies at all levels. The VUCA world unfolds itself against the backdrop of fog, clutter and lack of information, aptly described by Donald Rumsfeld as a world of *"unknown unknowns"* – what we don't know we don't know.

Developing leadership talent to cope with an interconnected, complex, interdependent and non-linear world is extremely challenging, as it requires strategic vision, creativity and risk-taking to find practical answers. These are life-skills which teachers must impart to children in their school years.

The Changing Nature of Work

Manufacturing jobs have fallen by 30 percent. In 1964, the American giant AT&T was worth $267 billion in today's dollar rate, and employed 7,58,611 persons. In 2015, Google was worth $ 370 billion, but employs a mere 55,000 employees – one-tenth of AT&T.

The very nature of jobs is changing. It is estimated that at the end of every decade, about 50 percent of existing jobs will become obsolete. Some estimates suggest that close to two billion jobs will disappear by 2030, including traditional schools and teachers to which we have been accustomed. Reskilling will thus be the order of the day as classical careers and professions will be a phenomenon of the past.

Two billion jobs will disappear by 2030, including the traditional schools and teachers to which we have been accustomed.

In another ten years everyone will be replaceable. Irrespective of what scenario plays out for human survival, lifelong learning will remain a master skill. Reskilling will be less about educational qualifications, and more about competencies, about hands-on experiences. In a world driven by artificial-thinking and machine-thinking, coding, math skills and empathy are the lingua franca of the 21st century.

Coding, math skills and empathy are the lingua franca of the 21st century.

Today, we often equate position with success. Climbing the position-ladder, from a junior executive to CEO may be less relevant in an industry driven by innovation. Employees will be paid and respected for ideas and not managing systems and processes. The concept of idea-meritocracy in decision-making is coming of age. Decision-making in an AI-dominated organization is unlikely to be based on autocracy and democracy. Instead, algorithms will drive collective decision-making with creative solutions.

Algorithms will drive collective decision-making with creative solutions.

Why We are not Creative

Undeniably, schools kill creativity, and most teachers are uncomfortable with children who are either over-curious, or ask too many questions. In hierarchical societies like India, children are trained to seek answers, and not ask questions. Traditional school education systems in most countries lack creativity because they emphasise scoring high marks in examinations to gain admission to renowned colleges. The fallout from lack of innovation in schools is alarming in the context of the innovation economy the world is living in.

In the past 72 years, India's Indian Institute of Science, Bangalore, and all the IITs (Indian Institutes of Technology) have not given the world a single invention. Unfortunately, the Indian system focuses on writing research papers but lacks core competencies required to implement them in real-life situations. In the Global Innovation Index of 2017, India is ranked 60, and only 17 percent of patents filed in India are from Indian individuals and companies. Moreover, in nearly 80 percent of the patent applications, it takes upto five years to obtain the patent. It is not, therefore, surprising that only 20 percent graduates from India's IITs are employable in MNCs and premier Indian companies.

In most schools, there is no serious attempt to instill creativity and thinking skills in students. As a result, by the time they become adults their creativity levels can drop to as low as 2 percent. In 1968, the renowned psychologist, Dr. George Land, administered a creative test to NASA scientists and engineers, as well as 1600 children from three to five years old. He re-tested the same children when they attained the age of 10 and 15. The results were outstanding:

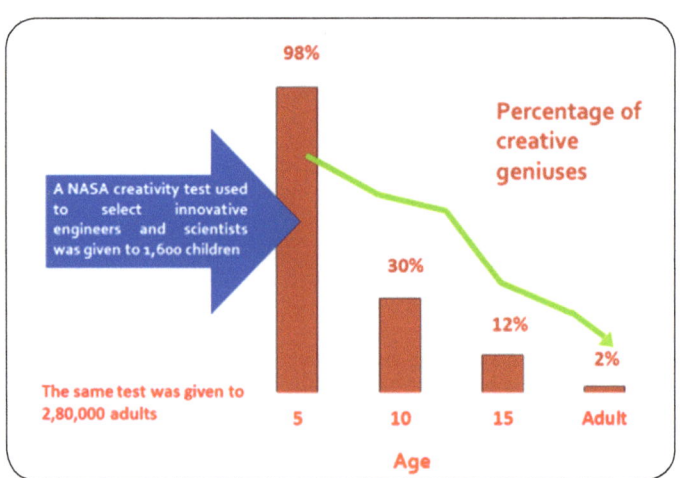

Creativity is also declining because of digital addiction, the large number of hours children spend watching TV, playing video games, and their obsession with high examination scores. Although pedagogically disputed, there is widespread belief amongst teachers, that creativity is a genetic talent reserved for only a few!

Another interesting study by the Organisation for Economic Co-operation and Development (OECD) in 2010, offered an interesting perspective on the relationship between math scores and perceived entrepreneurial capability of nations. Nations that had top scores in the Programme for International Student Assessment (PISA), were nations that ranked lowest in creativity.

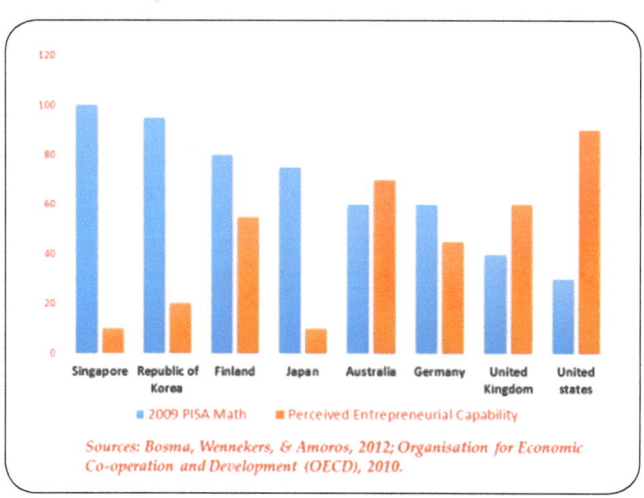

Sources: Bosma, Wennekers, & Amoros, 2012; Organisation for Economic Co-operation and Development (OECD), 2010.

Parents are risk-averse and overprotective of their children. Even Donald Trump. In the past he has deplored American football as a violent game. The President has made it clear he will not steer his son Barron to play American football as it is a *"dangerous sport."* In an interview, even President Barrack Obama said that, if he had a son, he would *"have to think long and hard"* to play American football because of the risk of injuries. Consequently, children are not risk-takers and critical thinkers essential for being innovative. Children are being mollycoddled and brought up in captivity by *"helicopter-parents."* They are afraid to play or go adventuring for fear of getting hurt or abused and prefer to sit at their computers, play stations and with mobile phones. Many parents want to bubble wrap their children to grow up in a sanitized environment.

Parents are risk-averse and overprotective of their children.

As children grown up they become more and more fearful of their environment. They are afraid to experiment, and unless we allow our children to fall (but not be failures) and rebound with grit, they will be ill-prepared to survive in the fiercely vicious dog-eats-dog world outside their cocooned lives. Educating parents (not students) on how to be less risk-averse is a challenge and is a book by itself.

Innovation is spurred by empathy, and empathy has been declining dangerously in the past 15 years. We are becoming more and more narcissistic, "me-minded," and lonelier than ever. Estimates put the decline to 40 percent among college students, who spend more time Googling than talking.

Empathy drives restlessness within a person to make a difference, to transform. Empathy starts with identity, which is derived from one's respect for one's people, one's culture, one's country, and the larger world. True identity arises through knowledge about one's country – not from abstraction. What you do not know you cannot respect.

Empathy drives restlessness within a person to make a difference, to transform. Empathy starts with identity.

Those who do not know much about their country cannot be expected to respect their country, and be empathetic.

Those who do not know much about their country cannot be expected to respect their country, and be determined to make a difference. This is explained schematically below:

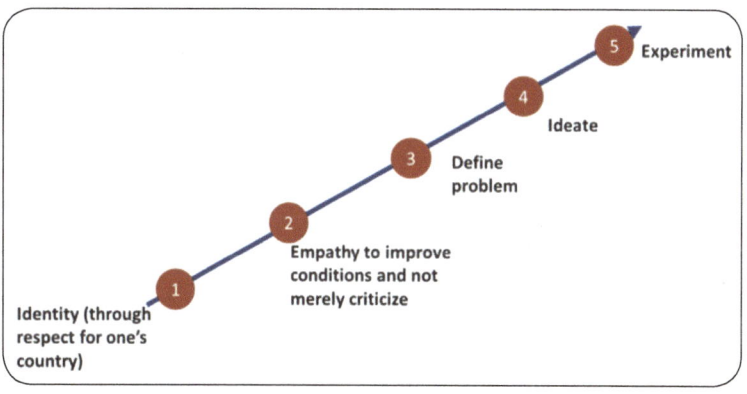

Culture of Schools is at Odds with Culture of Innovation

Creativity is a genetic gift because man is hardwired for creativity. Till children reach the age of five, their creative quotient is as high as 98 percent. Asian parenting style – the Tiger Mom variety, a hierarchical social and family structure, and flawed educational system, fosters conformity, mediocrity, uniformity in thinking, and the absence of individuality and innovation. This has been happening ever since the invention of the Gutenberg printing press in the 15th century. The hard evidence is there for everyone to see.

>Schools prepare children for jobs and not for life.

>Schools kill creativity deliberately.

>Standardised testing.

>Teaching content over competencies.

>Children lack individuality and independent thinking.

>In the past 72 years, IITs and IIMs have not produced one life-altering innovation.

> 83 percent of patents registered in India are by foreigners (non-Indians).
>
> This explains why, according to Apple's co-founder Wozniak,
>
> *"There will be no big tech company in India."*

In order to transform ideas into innovation, critical thinking, risk-taking and coping with failure are vital. Regrettably, the education system is content-driven, and there is no attempt to develop life competencies to solve real-life problems. To make matters worse, parents and schools over-protect children.

Teachers genuinely believe that, their primary task is to teach a subject, and not the child. Teachers do not read and reflect. Therefore, assessments do not reflect real learning, and students are incapable of applying knowledge of learned facts and principles.

Creativity Can be Taught

There is a million dollar question on everyone's lips: can creativity be taught? The immediate answer is: creativity does not have to be taught; it has to be re-ignited. Man is born creative; but because of antipathetic environmental factors, like over-protection, fear of failures and disempowerment, the creative juices stop flowing.

There is another factor that goes unnoticed. Everyone is creative, but only a few are innovative. To be creative is to have ideas; to be innovative is to be capable of applying these ideas to solve real-life problems creatively, and/or transform society. To be innovative we need to possess companion skills and competencies such as:

Empathy.

Critical thinking.

Team playing.

Concept-mindedness.

System thinking (intuition).

Focus and mindfulness.

Grit and resilience to deal with failure.

Risk-taking.

Persuasive communication.

Interdisciplinary knowledge.

There are other prerequisites too.

Absence of Fear

The absence of fear is a prerequisite for innovation.

Dictatorial regimes and hierarchical structures, (even at home) are seldom innovative. Learning cannot happen in an environment where making mistakes is discouraged, where the zero-error syndrome is hanging over one's head like the sword of Damocles, and a situation, where asking questions and suggesting innovative alternatives are seen as dissidence and insubordination.

Fear is the greatest inhibitor to learning, creativity, and seeking happiness.

We are living in the age of paranoia, the widely believed perception that *"Everyone is out to get me."* A paranoid person genuinely believes that everybody is ganging up against him, that he is isolated, and that there is more bad than good in people. The combination of fake news, an emotive and repetitive media, cut-throat competition, rising stress levels due to modern lifestyle and loneliness, and increasing inequalities, are fuelling paranoia. Paranoia is an unfounded perception and belief, a delusion that someone is out to harm us.

Fear is the greatest inhibitor to learning, creativity, seeking happiness, searching for truth, reaching our potential and even finding God. Present-day schooling aims at placing a student in a college of his/her choice, and following it up with a highly paid job. Instead, schools must consider that, a key purpose of education is to understand fear, and how to be free of it. Only then can an awakened mind be created, only then can creativity flourish. History testifies that authoritarian and hierarchical societies are seldom innovative. This has greater relevance in all-inclusive schools that admit students with varying learning abilities.

A key purpose of education is to understand fear.

There is no place for fear anywhere – in classrooms, at home and in society. Our entire approach to disciplining children must change. Threats, ridicule, sarcasm, intimidation and physical punishment are counter-productive. Of the myriad strategies to eliminate fear in classrooms, the following have stood the test.

1. The classrooms must be well-lit, clean and inviting. All physical spaces in the classrooms and corridor should display content to motivate learning. We may describe this as the **third teacher**.

2. **Student autonomy** in taking responsibility for their learning. Self-directed learning that precedes classroom learning is one of the most effective antidotes to indiscipline and boredom. The greater the devolution of learning, more the learning is effected.

3. **Conceptual understanding** holds the key to learning and discipline. This is not an easy task. If a teacher cannot explain a concept to an eight year old, it is very likely that the teacher does not understand the concept herself.

4. Conceptual understanding must be followed up by explaining the **relevance** of what is being learnt – the 'why' of what is being learnt, and how such learning can be applied usefully in our daily life.

5. **Personalization** of learning, to meet the pedagogical and emotional needs of individual students This flows out from the larger concept of what the role of the teacher should be: to teach the child and not the subject alone, thereby unlocking human potential.

6. Encourage **independent thinking** and **questioning** by:

    Asking open-ended questions that compel students to think and answer.

    Train students how to frame questions.

    Never belittling a question however unintelligent, naïve or stupid it may sound.

7. Use the **design-thinking process** to teach a subject, as it is an effective collaborative way to develop innovation-mindedness.

Inclusivity

Learning in all schools is designed for the average child. That explains why admissions are given on the basis of age-appropriateness. Given the scientific reality of brain plasticity, the concept of an average child is a myth. Everyone is special and different in their own way. Everyone has a personalised learning profile: memory, reading ability, language, knowledge, curiosity, and specific competencies, whatever.

Education should aim at personalising learning, thus providing equal opportunities to each child. Unfortunately, we design the learning curriculum for the average student without any emphasis on competencies required to succeed and flourish in the 21st century.

As a result of faulty designing, teachers are unable to unlock the child's potential. This notion of the average destroys talent. In the US, for example, about 4 percent of all school drop-outs – that is a staggering 50,000 kids, are intellectually gifted! Instead of personalising learning, we do what is natural: blame the child, the teacher or even the parent for a child's poor performance.

Inclusivity is about nurturing creativity and talent.

Books can be written about great statesmen, scientists, inventors, artists, actors, Nobel laureates, sportspersons and CEOs, who suffered from a learning disability. Today they would have been denied admission to the premier schools of the world. But for their creativity, the world would have been a poorer place.

Their story and contribution to humankind is a narrative of human apathy, an indictment of our education system, and above all a powerful message that disability is creative. Despite all the technology and science of Artificial Intelligence, we have yet to change the education system that is designed for the average, the so-called 'normals.'

Disability is creative.

Asking Creative Questions

The innovation culture begins with asking good questions. Good questions are questions that stimulate creative thinking. Those who are afraid of asking questions or raising their eyebrows, can never be creative. It's a well-documented fact that schools discourage children from asking questions.

Children and adults who ask questions become better thinkers, more creative and better problem solvers. You start dying the day you stop asking questions as a child, as a student and

You start dying the day you stop asking questions.

as a citizen. You also stop being curious about life and the environment you live in.

Between the ages of 2 and 5, children ask about 40,000 questions. Thereafter, they stop asking questions because schools discourage children asking questions. Teachers and examinations want only answers. What they do not realise is that one gets good answers only when one asks good questions.

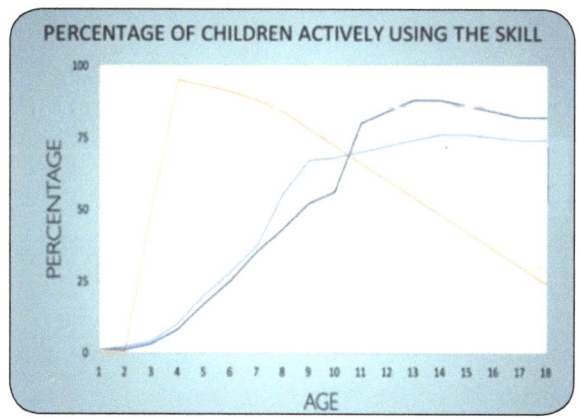

Teachers must be trained in the technique of designing good questions, and should practise it while delivering their lessons. With experience, the following sequence has paid off handsomely:

- Teacher asks *'think-time* questions' having a wait-time of about 7 seconds to reflect and respond. The questions are such that children are compelled to pause and think before replying, thereby improving their critical thinking skills and quality of answers. Instead of asking what the capital of India is, the teacher asks, why should a country have a capital? Why not separate political and financial capitals?

- Teachers must be trained in the question formulation technique, and should practise it on a regular basis. The methodology is simple:

Teacher sets the focus.

Students are made to understand the difference between closed questions, and the power of open-ended questions.

Students are encouraged to ask as many questions as they want.

The teacher helps students to prioritise the bucket list.

Students reflect or brainstorm.

Self-Directed Learning

Self-directed and interdependent learning is one of the best forms of training for creativity. The responsibility for learning shifts from the teacher to the student – student-centred learning. It is the only form of learning which combines application of content, plus competencies to solve problems creatively.

Self-directed and interdependent learning is one of the best forms of training for creativity.

The following **6-step** process will help in developing the habit of self-learning:

1. Teacher identifies the:

    Concepts and their relevance.

    Divergent views on concepts.

    Possible areas of application.

    Aspects of the concept, which Google cannot teach.

2. Students are taught how to learn the specific lesson – a significant departure from the linear pipeline model where

students are mere consumers of knowledge. Now they are able to create their own knowledge – an act of creativity.

3. Students ask questions vis-à-vis each concept for clarification and understanding.
4. Students develop content around each question. Could be a peer effort.
5. Self-assessment.
6. Teacher reviews lesson.

The above process ensures the development of the following competencies necessary for the 21st century:

Independent learning.

Creativity and critical thinking.

Self-efficacy and self-esteem.

Lifelong learning.

Liberal Education

Liberal education is not the same as liberal arts. Liberal arts is a sub set of liberal education. Even a science college can provide liberal education. Traditional education prepares students to pass examinations and get a good job. Liberal education prepares one for life and for one's sixth job! In a political context, a liberal is one who is opposed to conservatism and orthodoxy. However, in leadership, being liberal-minded has different connotations. A liberal-minded person is a practitioner of:

Learning how to learn.

Independent thinking.

Caring.

Openness to change.

Creative.

In an AI-driven world of automation and machine-thinking, liberal education is assuming greater importance by the day. The only way we can compete with computers and humanoids is by becoming aware of our inner world – to manage our thoughts, emotions and feelings, and thereby expand our consciousness. Liberal education enables us to do precisely that.

Liberal education does not just develop abilities; it discovers abilities by unlocking potential through:

> *Liberal education does not just develop abilities.*

- A higher purpose that gives man a vision and meaning to life, and makes him self-aware in the process. This is the pinnacle in Maslow's Hierarchy of Needs.
- Values that help us in governing our life and exercising choices.
- Freedom from biases and prejudices.
- Resilience and grit in the face of adversity and failure.
- Competencies to cope with the challenges of a VUCA world.
- Becoming a citizen who thinks globally and acts locally.

Liberal education is the application of knowledge by developing specific competencies to be able to apply them in real-life situations. This is creativity. In a classroom situation the emphasis is no longer on content but on:

- Understanding its relevance and context.
- Extracting main ideas and concepts and their application.

Focusing on the heart and mind, and not the head alone.

Self-directed learning to the maximum extent possible as this helps in application to solve problems.

The purpose of art in schools requires a complete re-think. Art in school, in any form, is not to turn a child into a Picasso, but to develop the thinking and habits of an artist such as:

Deliberate practice.

Discipline and sacrifices required for achieving mastery and excellence.

Self-awareness and understanding of one's emotions, feelings and thoughts.

Humanist education was thought at the time (the renaissance in Europe) to be an important factor in the preparation of life. Its main goal was to improve the lives of citizens and help their communities. This need, if anything, has now become magnified. Natural, political and other disasters leave in their wake, tragedy, loss and confusion. Human resilience must be strengthened, *en masse,* through education, innovation and indefatigable and indomitable human endeavour.

Chapter 6

Learning to Lead

Most leaders talk and write nostalgically about what they achieved in life, in work, and how they went about it. Or, they advise everyone on how to lead. Very, very few share their thoughts and experiences about the way they learned to lead. I am still learning to lead, a process that will never cease, because being a leader means self-awareness and leading oneself first, and then others.

Industrial Age thinking and 38 years' service in the army nurtured me on the command and control model of leadership – hierarchical, trait and situation-based style leadership. Moreover, leadership was male-dominated and associated with job positions, power and wealth. The advance of globalisation in India in the mid-90s, the information revolution and success in foiling insurgency in Ladakh, changed my world-view on leadership.

My life was transformed when I underwent a crucible, life-altering experience in early 2000. I was then commanding 14 Corps in Ladakh. To prevent insurgency from spilling across the Kashmir Valley, I launched a mass socio-political movement – *Operation Sadbhavna* – to win over alienated communities. The gun was never used; and we brought peace to the region in as short a time as six months. Eighteen years have since elapsed and Ladakh remains a zone of peace. The 21 months I spent in Ladakh also witnessed the greatest growth in my emotional personality and spiritual self.

Three realizations came to me: one, leadership is about self-awareness—leading myself first, then others; two, life must have a higher purpose; and three, as life per se does not have any meaning, we have to give meaning to life. As a result, I left the army prematurely to try and make a difference to society through quality international education.

From a leadership perspective, *Sadbhavna* made me realize (though late in life) that, leadership is the art of leading oneself first, then others. The traditional models of leading I had been practicing for 55 years were restrictive in scope, and externalized leadership as character traits and values. It was about controlling and influencing the outer environment. Traditional leadership models can be summarized as under:

Newtonian — Man is materialistic and his behaviour is deterministic. As a consequence, leadership is founded upon certain laws and principles. Such a view ignores the randomness of life and its chaotic nature.

Darwinian — Life is a struggle where only the fittest will survive; and therefore, dogs will eat dogs and winning is everything – collaboration be damned.

Market-Driven — What matters are profits; values are not important. Such a leadership philosophy dismisses outright, a moral truth – that means are as important as the ends. Moreover, the aim of business cannot be only to become rich. Business must plough back some of its profits to improve the quality of the life of its employees, the community and the environment. Indian business schools and Indian business leaders, with some notable exceptions of the likes of Azim Premji and Shiv Nadar, continue to be driven by market profits.

The successful campaign in preventing conflict in Ladakh gave rise to a second awakening within me – **the transformative power of crucible experiences**. There are two kinds of experiences one encounters. The first is of low psychological intensity, and brings about a change only to the extent that it makes an individual more effective – a better manager, a better parent, a better citizen.

The second kind of experience is crucible and life-altering, a derivative from the days of alchemists. The belief was that when heated to high temperatures, all base metals turn into gold. Crucibles are thus unplanned defining moments that can be events, episodes, stages in life, relationships, traumas or revelations that transform an individual. The individual reinvents himself – gains a new identity, a new vision, a new mission in life.

In the ancient period, the ruthless Maurya ruler Ashok, underwent a major transformation as a man of peace as a result of the gruesome Battle of Kalinga. So did Buddha, who renounced the world and his princely title on being deeply affected by the suffering of his subjects. In recent history, Gandhi experienced this when he was thrown off the train for sharing a seat with a European in a first-class compartment on June 7, 1893, when travelling from Durban to Pretoria. Mandela's great transformation in pursuing peace and reconciliation happened as a result of his imprisonment in Robben Island. Despite enduring torture and brutality for 27 years, Mandela's will and spirit of forgiveness could never be broken. He finally left prison as a man of peace – peace between the Blacks and the Whites of his country, peace for the rest of the world.

Crucible experiences need not be only personal ones; they could be those of others as well. We find them in books. We extract them and sensitize ourselves by deep reading and deep thinking.

Leader Training Starts Early

Age is no barrier to becoming a leader, nor is leadership a competency reserved only for the elders in society. Values and concepts of life and mind are learnt by the age of eight or nine; and therefore, parents need to appreciate that it is they who are primarily responsible for leadership training of their children.

In my formative years, my parents were not able to spend time on my leadership development. Consequently, on becoming a parent, I resolved that I would prepare my children to lead right from the start. However, for the better part of my children's schooling and college education I was serving at the borders; and it was not possible to formally organize personal growth and leadership development of our children in the manner we understand today. This is also the fate of everyone who is living and working 24x7. So I settled for the next best strategy:

- Rather than preaching to my children, I set ethical standards in conduct and core values. While role-modelling, we need to be on guard that children must never mimic their parents. They lose their individuality in the process. Role-modelling must inspire children to chase their own dream to become what they can and, should be.

- Nurturing their talent and encouraging them to pursue a career they were passionate about. Our son was a budding artist, and we said to him, *"Son, focus on your art. You have great talent. As long as you pass in other subjects, it's ok with us."* Today we never regret that decision. Being in the middle of the class is OK as long as one's grades are acceptable. This provides free time and opportunity to learn other skills and competencies in becoming entrepreneurs and innovators.

This thinking is at odds with the traditional belief that, to come first in the class is the end-all and be-all of life.
- Fostering the reading habit by making them lifelong learners, by sharing with them what we read.

Role-modeling is the key in leadership development of children. A boy, when reminded not to use an unacceptable four-letter word had this to say: *"My parents use it, their friends too. My favorite film and TV stars are using it all the time. If it was all that bad, then why should they be using it in the first place?"*

Higher Purpose – Man's Ultimate Motivation

Sadbhavna was a crucible experience that transformed me, and kick-started my journey to seek a higher purpose. As the journey commenced, two important questions loomed large on my mind: who am I, and what am I here for?

I realized that life must have a meaning other than merely living, and a higher purpose, that goes beyond power, position and wealth. Thus, the sole purpose of my life could not be to become a General in the army; that would destroy my authenticity as an empowered individual. *"What is the meaning of life?"* is not a philosophical question or a religious one. Rather, it is personal; about the meaning an individual gives to his life. As a result, no one should be saying that his understanding of meaning is right and everyone else's is wrong. All meanings of life and higher purposes are justifiable as long as they flow out from one's world view.

Life must have a meaning other than merely living.

The higher purpose is transcendental, like implementing the will of God, or pursuing a cause (such as preserving the environment), an ideology like political autonomy, or making a difference in the lives of people beyond one's immediate family. A higher purpose gives one a reason to live and presents a challenge that places heavy demands on sacrificing what is most valuable to a person. It is through the pursuit of a higher purpose that self-awareness and happiness arise within us, and we give meaning to life. Winston Churchill once said, *"We make a living by what we get, but we make a life by what we give."*

> *We make a living by what we get, but we make a life by what we give.*

Seeking a higher purpose does not demand a change in lifestyle from a common person to an ascetic, or detachment from worldly chores, or wearing the coarse robe of a monk. Nor are desires, passions and egoism impediments. One can live and enjoy the outer world, and yet be able to pursue a higher purpose—a spiritual path. Man's outer and inner lives can be lived together.

The Need for a Guru

The concept of a guru or a spiritual guide, is an oriental tradition enshrined in Hinduism, Buddhism, and Sikhism. In a Western sense, the closest meaning of a guru is a mentor, or an enlightened one. But there is a difference. An enlightened person knows the truth but may not be able to communicate it to others. A guru, a spiritual guide or a master can. An enlightened one has answers, but only the master can explain why and how he has arrived at these answers. The guru's primary role is to help a person answer the question, who am I? Unless we know ourselves, we are unable to understand the universe, even God.

> *An enlightened one has answers, but only the master can explain why and how he has arrived at these answers.*

J Krishnamurti and Swami Vivekananda, were known for their "anti-guru" views. They believed that man did not need the guidance of a guru to attain self-realization. Man does not have to search for God because God is within us – *Ahambrahmasmi*. J Krishnamurti often emphasized that there never was any one path to Truth. There are several paths and each individual must find his own. While he is intellectually right, for common persons like me, the journey towards self-awareness would inevitably be slow and delayed. Moreover, in a high-paced world, the tensions of daily life, economic necessities and pleasures are distracting; they impede us from choosing an independent path. As I mentioned earlier, the greatest spurt in my emotional and spiritual growth occurred after the age of 55. I only wish it had happened much earlier, and had someone to guide me. Instead, I had to study, struggle, and reflect deeply to discover who I am, and to understand the world around me.

But then, gurus are difficult to find. Therefore, once you start becoming spiritually aware, don't wait for a guru to come because gurus are rare to find and will not come to you; you will have to go to them. Should one accept you, will you be prepared to surrender yourself totally? Thinking men and women can find this act self-abasing and disempowering.

While it is desirable to find a guru, the reality is otherwise. The search is individual and so others should not impose their path upon you. You and you alone have to follow an independent path because the Kingdom of God is within you. Remember, you have to be ready to walk down the road all alone and there are no short cuts. You become your own teacher; your own guru. Although the travelling time is longer, the very act of walking and struggling alone is enjoyable.

On Books and Spiritual Awakening

If you cannot find a guru, the next best thing is to read his books. Paul Brunton once wrote,

> *"Every book which stimulates aspiration and widens reflection does spiritual service and acts as a guru."*
>
> *– Paul Brunton*

Books are of great help to those who become their own teachers. The only problem with books on spirituality and philosophy is that since their texts are coded, the help of a guru, an evolved person, or deep reflection, may be necessary to deconstruct their content.

I have always had a passion for books ever since I was a young officer serving at the borders. Even while patrolling close to the Line of Control in Kashmir, I would carry a minimum of two books in my rucksack. When we harboured for the night, I would light a candle inside the pup-tent, read, and make notes. If there was no paper, I would write on the smooth surface of the bark of silver birch trees that grew abundantly at heights of 9,500 feet and above.

Books contain the distilled crucible experiences of great leaders and enlightened masters. So do scriptures and books on spirituality. To discount them would be foolish, as one would lose out on different perspectives of life. For example, the holy books of all religions contain the wisdom of prophets and sagacious men and women. In Sikhism, the holy book, the Guru Granth Sahib, is deemed the eleventh guru of the Sikhs. What better learning can anyone receive!

Of all the experiences we undergo, 80 percent are those of other people, or indirect experiences. They are contained in scriptures, books and lectures and are equally rich and transformational. However, in order to benefit from them, one has to be evolved to a certain level to be able to understand them. Scriptures, for example, are coded. Common persons read the content literally, and therefore, focus more on the rituals. The evolved, on the other hand, "deconstruct" the meaning at a spiritual plane.

Books have greatly influenced me in my journey towards self-awareness. I spend a lot of time researching to select books across a wide array of topics, and annotate the pages as I read the content.

After reading a book, I make notes on the main concepts, themes and viewpoints of the author. I often revisit the books and notes I have made; then reflect on the central ideas and concepts, and how I can apply them in my life, in my organization. To read a book without reflection is as good as not reading the book. Revisiting is important because one may not understand the author in the first or even second reading. J Krishnamurti's writings are one such example that comes easily to my mind.

Concepts of Life

Understanding and practising concepts of life are central to unlearning and transformational leadership. My interest in concepts was ignited by studies of the Vietnam War. During negotiations on exchange of prisoners of war, the leader of the American delegation asked the North Vietnamese general, *"Can you cite one example of where the American forces lost any battle?"* The North Vietnamese replied, *"You may be right, but you lost the war."* It is a human failing that we are forever trying to score tactical victories over others in life, in work, and in relationships. The truth is that one can win all the battles in life, and yet lose the war. For leaders, winning the war is more important.

Understanding and practising concepts of life are central to unlearning and transformational leadership.

A concept is an abstract idea like 'God' and 'work,' that helps us to understand the world and ourselves, and gives us purpose and direction in life. This is best illustrated with the example of work.

Is the concept of work aimed at earning money, or finding personal fulfillment by linking one's work with a higher goal? The reader will remember the janitor who told President John Kennedy that, he was part of a team that was putting man on the moon?

Fulfillment can also arise when the work is so enjoyable that the individual experiences transform into 'flow' – a meditative state of mind when all sense of time vanishes, and all other thoughts go away. Or is the concept of work Calvinian, which believes in the idea of *predestination,* namely, that human salvation lies in becoming a select member of the Elect, persons who are chosen by God to go to heaven? Calvinism advocates that work is the will of God and all profits must be reinvested again and again. Poverty is thus a punishment for idleness, and wealth is a reward for hard work. So let us become rich and even richer as quickly as possible. This concept of work epitomizes the market philosophy, *"I consume, therefore, I am."* Depending on which concept of work one believes in, one's mission in life and values will be determined accordingly.

A key finding in neuroscience is that concepts of life, mind and matter are learned in the early years; thereafter the degree of difficulty in learning increases with age. The lack of concept teaching is a serious flaw in home and school education. As a result, although a child may score high marks in examinations, she is unable to apply her school learning in real-life situations. The challenge for teachers is that concepts have to be written, explained and demonstrated age-appropriately. The younger the child, the more difficult it is. For example, how do we explain to a child of four what or who God?

A leader's ability to conceptualise problems and issues is largely due to the habit of extensive reading, the study of classics on a wide variety of subjects, and reflecting on what she reads. These range from conflict to religion, philosophy, human learning, neuroscience, psychology and history – a fair mix of the liberal arts, humanities and sciences. The study of classics and original works bring forth the author's thought processes and the 'why' of what was done or what was said. Another useful source are biographies, autobiographies, and the crucible and experiential lessons from the lives of other people.

Effective and empowered leaders must acquire deep understanding and practise their key concepts of life. For example, the reader will find the following concepts useful in leading their lives:

- Reverence for life.
- Higher purpose.
- Spirituality vis a vis religion.
- Innate goodness of human beings.
- Life is beautiful despite its ugly side.
- Love and forgiveness.
- Work.
- Lifelong learning

Concepts are usually trans-disciplinary and holistic, and unlike those of mind and matter, are universal, and unlikely to change. Till the age of forty-five, my trans-disciplinary capability was restricted mainly to the military sphere of warfare. This was disconcerting, as the military domain had narrowed my life's vision. Overnight, I gave up reading military books; and switched over to a generous menu of non-fiction books on varied subjects from science to liberal arts to human behavior, to human security. For over four decades now this passion continues with unabated fervor.

Folk Traditions

There are two worlds that co-exist – the outer and the inner world. Both have different laws, different realities, different perceptions and different possibilities.

For the past millennium, the focus in education has been in controlling the outer world of materialism; of nature; of resources of the planet – gold, water, oil, minerals; and people. Hence the emphasis on science, mathematics and pedagogy of the head. This has all changed overnight. We are now at the start off the 4th Industrial Age, dominated by Artificial Intelligence, deep-thinking and innovation. In this new environment, there is a pronounced shift towards education of the inner world – the world of happiness, meaning, compassion, innovation and emotions.

The purpose of education should be *"to educate both the heart and the mind and not the brain alone, in order to prepare a child to be a lifelong learner, to give meaning to life, and unlock human potential to succeed in a VUCA world."*

This necessitates a shift: from teaching content, to teaching entrepreneurial competencies – for application of knowledge to solve problems creatively.

In today's digital world, acceleration is increasing; empathy is going downhill; we do not have any time to pause and reconnect with ourselves and our dear ones; and globalization is slowing down. In this scenario, we need a new operative environment to manage the inner world, and nurture innovation.

We believe that folk art and aesthetic traditions – the language of the heart and mind, will be the nucleus of this operative environment that will focus on:

1. Localism – think global but act local.
2. Identity – my roots; my culture.
3. Innovation – the belief that man is born potential; with intrinsic motivation, a positive environment and deliberate practice, he becomes talent. The Manganiar singing community from the desert of Rajasthan is an example.

A key aspect of folk traditions (and even innovation) that has gone unnoticed lies in the power of hands. There are more connections between the palm and the brain than any other body part.

Gandhi role-modelled spinning and weaving, not because it provided employment, but because he believed that, craft-centric education had great value in developing leadership:

Self-expression.

Individualism.

Creative stimulation.

Dignity of human beings.

Servant-leadership – serve first, and lead second.

Spiritual and emotional development.

Strategic Culture and Sense of History

One is fascinated by history and futurism. History is not just a story of the past, but a projection of the past onto the screen of the future, about what could happen tomorrow. How do we interpret the past to make sense of the future? As early as the 1930s, H G Wells spoke about the need for setting up Departments and Professors of Foresight in universities. A sense of history provides a leader with foresight and existential intelligence – the ability to look beyond the horizon.

History is not a story of the past, but a projection of the past onto the screen of the future, about what could happen tomorrow.

High IQ scores are not indicative of an individual's or a nation's strategic culture. The recent fall of America, Inc. should set us thinking. The United States is a world leader in knowledge capital, an assembly of the best brains in the world, and a military and economic superpower. So, we all thought. This has changed in the last decade.

The cognitive powerhouses of the United States gave the world the very powerful idea of growth rates. Despite deficits, it became the mantra of economic prosperity. Then everything changed drastically, overnight. One trillion dollars were wiped out in stock markets in one day, starting the world's greatest financial meltdown.

Justifying the Iraq war in the name of promoting democracy is seen by the world as hegemonistic. As Francis Fukuyama wrote in the Newsweek edition of 13 October 2008, *"…by using democracy to justify the Iraq war, the Bush administration suggested to many that, "democracy" was a code for military intervention and regime change."* Add to this state-sponsored torture in Guantanamo Bay and Abu Ghraib; and therefore the question: "What happened to IQ?"

The American idea of Ronald Reagan's market capitalism found complete acceptance by Wall Street, World Bank and the International Monetary Fund. De-regulation, minimum government interference, and enjoying high growth rates despite deficits became the mantras of economic prosperity.

Why did American IQ pay no heed to warning signs – the Asian financial crisis of 1997–98, and staggering deficits of $700 billion a year by 2007?

A possible explanation: When dogma dictates politics and economics, there is little room for "big picture" and flexible thinking. When arrogance arises, strategy takes a back seat, and raw power replaces 'soft' power by insisting on having one's way, believing it to be the superior way, the only way. Arrogance has the habit of shutting one's ears to what others are saying. Vision and judgment are the first casualties.

To Lead, Serve First

A leader must serve before he can lead himself or herself. The very act of service develops one's emotional and spiritual quotient, thus helping one to become aware of oneself. My first lesson in service came from the military credo epitomized by Field Marshall Philip Chetwode's advice: *"The safety, honour and welfare of your country come first, always and every time. The honour, welfare and comfort of the men you command come next. Your own ease, comfort and safety come last, always and every time."*

Military service is a constant reminder that, if we expect a soldier in war to die for country and flag, the soldiers must be looked after in times of peace. As a young Captain, I spent two large spells of my annual leave trekking in the Kumaon Hills, meeting soldiers on leave and their families from my Regiment. This afforded me a deep insight into the minds and aspirations of the men I was commanding.

The major experience in servant leadership for me came as a Corps Commander at the age of 56, when I fought incipient insurgency by winning the population over. Success was achieved by providing high quality service – health care, elementary education, ICT and women's empowerment, and making the populace feel they were wanted.

The concept of service is not easily understood. Service is not about raising money for a cause, signing cheques, making an app to connect people to a task, or providing vocational opportunities for livelihood. These measures are laudable; but not enough. The idea of service goes well beyond and is an expression of one's love, humility and servanthood – like Jesus washing the feet of his disciples or Gandhi cleaning the common toilets in his ashram in South Africa. Service is all about using one's hands!

Intuitive Judgment

Looking back at life, I see that all major judgments in my personal and professional life have been correct – delaying my graduation by one year in favour of visiting New Zealand as a debater, choice of military career, marriage, my first book criticizing army and government policy in Kashmir, conflict prevention in Ladakh, and leaving the army prematurely to take up international education. These judgments were intuitive and taken with little or no advice – what is now called system 1 thinking.

Judgment and decision-making are dependent on several attributes a leader ought to possess. These are (apart from intuition) caused by:

- A deep sense of history and inter-disciplinary knowledge that enables the leader to do 'big-picture' thinking, and be able to see life beyond the immediate horizon.

- Concept thinking that facilitates understanding of problems and finding appropriate solutions.

- Being able to make sense of one's experiences. Experiences by themselves are of little use unless they can be interpreted and useful lessons drawn in order to change oneself.

- The power of execution. Good judgments are meaningless unless they are executed through a ferocity of purpose. Moreover, the efficacy of any sound judgment is also dependent on how the leader shares his/her vision, shaping the environment, often the re-education of followers, and personal presence.

Bisexuality or Androgyny

From commanding soldiers for 38 years, overnight I found myself (still am) leading a women dominant organization – schools, where women comprise nearly 90 percent of the school teacher population, at least in India. When this changeover took place in April 2002, globalization had gathered momentum in India. From a leadership perspective this set me thinking on the subject of androgyny. I soon realized that I had suppressed a lot of the femininity within myself in my military years, and had forgotten that human beings are bi-sexual – half man, half woman. In Hinduism, Lord Shiva is called *ardhanarishwara* because he symbolizes bisexuality.

To succeed in the 21st century, leaders will need to draw on their masculine and feminine traits (hitherto suppressed). Unfortunately, men go through life suppressing their femininity and women their masculinity. There is even another tragedy. Men even suppress some aspects of their manhood while women do likewise with womanhood. According to Freud, this gives rise to neurosis and lack of completeness in individuals. Only when the two integrate into one is the whole leader born. Men and women have a lot to learn from each other. The ideal gender competency combination is to select the best from both sexes.

Leaders will need to draw on their masculine and feminine traits (hitherto suppressed).

The ideal gender competency combination is shown below.

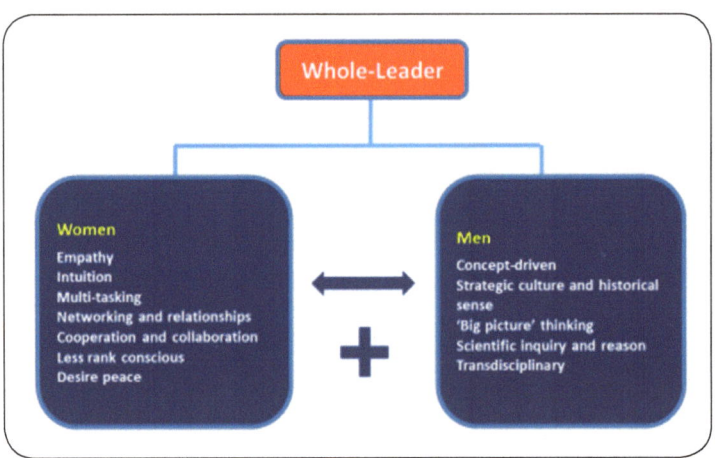

Becoming Whole

Wholeness in a personality evolves when we invest valuable time in the self, at work, in the home and in the community. Till the age of fifty, my total time investments were in work and family. As a result of my Ladakh experience (after the age of fifty-five), I added 'community' to the equation. Overnight my world-view and self-awareness expanded, and I added the fourth dimension – self.

My understanding of balance and wholeness has improved as a result of a SWOT analysis, but with a difference. As opposed to the traditional SWOT exercise management schools teach, I regularly conduct two simple tasks:

- One, a SWOT analysis each in the domains of home, profession, self and community.
- Two, I believe that to be whole, the masculinity and femininity of an individual must integrate into one. So I ask myself two questions:
- What aspects of femininity am I suppressing?
- Are there some aspects of my masculinity that I am not expressing explicitly?

Thereafter, I include the results of these two exercises in a SWOT chart. Now a clear picture emerges of how imbalanced I am, and what possible measures I need to take to redress this imbalance.

An authentic leader is a whole-person, a balanced individual. To be balanced does not mean that all four circles of life overlap. That is a myth and will seldom happen. The emphasis will keep on changing depending upon which stage of life one is at; yet the circles are compatible and not in conflict. In my instance the progression is shown below schematically.

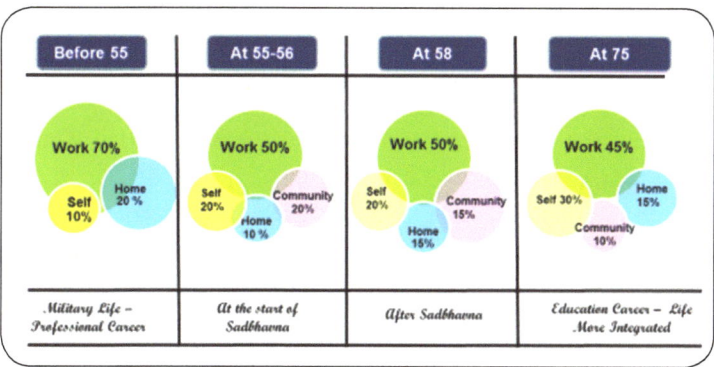

My experience in becoming whole brings out four lessons:

- First, the concept of self and community arose very late in life because of a crucible experience closer to the age of fifty five. This experience – the Sadbhavna experience – started the process of self-awareness and transformation within me.

- Second, I led an imbalanced existence during my professional career, spanning 37 years. Work took over-riding precedence at the cost of the family and community.

- Third, while the emphasis in each circle will vary in accordance with one's particular stage in life, and the expectations of one's key stakeholders, balance demands that all four circles must overlap for better results in professional goals, giving meaning to work, fostering better relationships, pursuing a higher purpose, becoming self-aware and experiencing happiness.

- Herman Hesse's novel *Journey to the East* has reinforced my unshakable belief, that, service in any form makes one disciplined and less egoistic. Those who live their lives for others, live and lead. This explains why children must be initiated into community service as early as possible.

Failure Is the Best Teacher

Failures led me to improve upon my leadership abilities, quality of thinking and creativity. Most people are afraid of failing, and can go to ridiculous extents to prevent failures. This mentality develops what is called the zero-error syndrome, an aversion to risk-taking and absence of innovation.

A lot of my success would never have been possible, but for the big failures I experienced in being able to motivate many to:

Give meaning to their lives, by pursuing a higher purpose.

Designing their future and sense of belonging, by following a vision.

Being innovative and critical-thinkers.

Becoming lifelong learners through the habit of deep reading.

But I have no regrets! I have gotten into the habit of getting excited even at the prospect of failing, because I have realised three home truths:

One: failures in life and at work teach us more than success. Failure is the best teacher, the best antiseptic to life's problems.

Two: innovation is the #1 leadership competency in today's Fourth Industrial Age. Innovation is all about risk-taking and creativity. Besides, there is no better way of developing grit and resilience to survive in a VUCA world. Only failure nurtures our grit.

Three: I value imperfections of human beings, of life, of people, of myself as necessary conditions for growth and happiness. I realise that perfection is undesirable. That the only perfect person is an imperfect person; so is nature; so is the cycle of life and death.

True love is love for others' imperfection.

That our beauty lies in our imperfections because beauty is imperfect, impermanent and incomplete. That true love is, love for others' imperfections.

Each one of us is unique and special and we learn differently. What is common, however, is that to be able to lead oneself, there has to be self-awareness.

I am still learning to lead. Every day is a lesson in learning and in leading oneself. Man's quest for self-awareness through crucible experiences, deep reflection, and making a difference, wherever he is, is his story of leadership and salvation. The journey is slow, bumpy, and often painful and frustrating; a journey that each individual must design and execute on his/her own. This burning desire to transform oneself has to come from within.

Chapter 7

Measuring the Impact of Leadership

My fundamental premise in leadership development is that, self-development is a precondition for professional development. It is, therefore, imperative to measure the impact of one's leadership development.

Only a few organisations measure the impact of leadership development that aims at self-growth. While it is relatively easy to measure cognitive abilities, skills, techniques, goal-setting, positivity and persuasive communication, it is indeed very difficult to assess the spiritual and higher emotional quotient of a person. For example, how can we evaluate the levels of self-awareness in an individual, or whether he has found meaning in life, or the intensity and genuineness of higher order emotions like compassion, reverence for life, and love?

Self-development is a precondition for professional development.

These attributes are intangible and therefore difficult to measure. Their measurement is beyond the capability of ordinary mortals, however successful they may have been as leaders. The one who evaluates has to be an evolved person in the first place. At best, one can give broad traffic-light assessments: red for a person who is devoid of these abilities, green for one who possesses them, and orange for a person who is a border-line case. When you work with people over time, a broad categorisation is possible.

Teacher Disposition

An effective teacher is one who is proficient in three professional abilities: knowledge of content, pedagogy for application of content, and teacher disposition. The first two are relatively easy to acquire; but teacher disposition is not.

Teacher disposition is the intrinsic motivation a teacher must have to unlock human potential, to teach the child and not just the subject, engage students, and make learning collegial and relevant. The second hypothesis is straight forward: Self-development is a precondition for professional development. Self-development makes a teacher mindful and can change her attitude to work – from mere teaching to a calling.

With a better understanding of the need for a personal vision, greater political social and cultural awareness, the leadership aspirations of Generation Y teachers can be met. Consequently, these factors must be addressed pro-actively if leadership development is to be effective.

Personal Vision

The success of leadership development begins with the pursuit of a personal vision, a vision that aims at one's moral growth and that of others. We confuse a personal vision with goals. Goals in business, in professions such as teaching, or for career, or for our biological children, are not personal goals. Likewise, a personal vision is different. The vision is about the self, about one's self-growth and contribution in four key dimensions – spiritual, emotional, cognitive and physical. The vision, therefore, looks at one's life holistically.

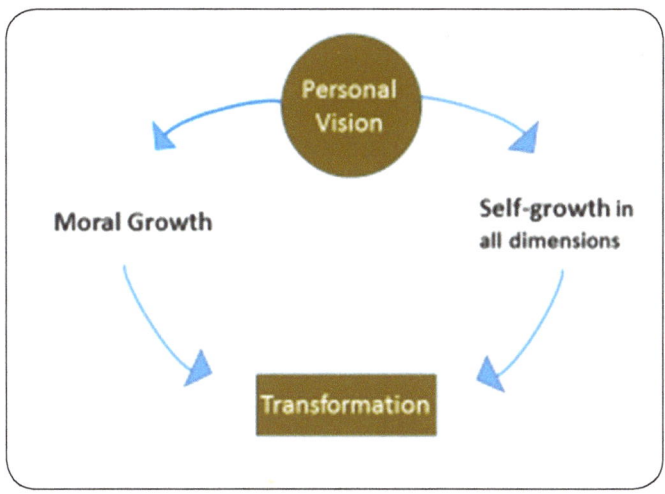

For the present, let us keep organizational visions aside. For any transformational leader, a personal vision is the start point. Without a vision, one's transformation cannot happen. Visionary leaders are visionary in their personal lives, and realise the critical need for organizational vision. Therefore, the vision journey begins with you. You cannot be a transformational leader if you cannot transform yourself first. And that will happen only, and only if you are a believer and practitioner of the power of vision.

A vision is a graphic 100 pixel picture of the desired end state of where and when an individual should be. While goals will change and will be modified because of the changing ground situation, the vision remains constant. A compelling vision is like a clarion call; it motivates individuals to action. The vision, therefore, should be inspirational, and unequivocally articulate the values that will guide the journey.

> *A vision is a graphic 100 pixel picture of the desired end state of where and when an individual should be.*

We live in an unknowable world. With each passing day the world is becoming more and more volatile, uncertain, complex, chaotic and ambiguous. Life, politics, economics, jobs, environment and relationships are all in a constant state of churning, and no one is sure what the final outcome will be. Even goals will change or require modification. Although everything will change, the only constant that will remain is man's vision, a vision of his or her desired future. One's personal vision enables a person to empower herself or himself, and take charge of one's life and destiny. To a large extent, a vision will also help a person to answer the obvious existential question in one's life.

- Who am I?
- How do I want to live?
- What do I wish to live for?
- What difference would I like to make?
- What legacy will I leave behind?

The answers to these questions form part of one's personal leadership vision; and in the long run, the impact of personal vision is infinitely greater than the success of an organizational vision.

Positivity

To be a transformational leader in the face of daunting challenges, one needs high self-esteem, along with a positive attitude towards life and work. By all accounts, close to 80 percent of us suffer from low self-esteem, and 87 percent do not find work fulfilling. Self-doubt, the expected arrival of the great redeemer, misinterpretation of *karmic* theory and the herd-mentality, are collectively responsible for the negativity we see in society.

There are historical reasons for Indians to have self-doubt, a mental condition wherein one doubts one's talent and capabilities, and lacks confidence to stand up and be counted, by asserting oneself. Centuries of foreign rule, particularly by the Mughals and the British, have been responsible for this psyche. Self-doubt is the enemy of positivity.

Teachers occupy positions of privilege because they are expected to touch the lives of the children they teach. They are potters who are molding clay and giving life to it. Students are plastic, they will turn out the way they are shaped. So why the self-doubt?

Throughout history we have been conditioned to believe that a messiah, or an iconic leader will one day appear on the scene and lead us out of our miseries into the promised land. Ours is a hierarchical society and nearly everyone is looking over their shoulder. This is epitomised in one of India's well known *bhajans* or devotional songs:

तेरा रामजी करेंगे बेड़ा पार

उदास मन काहेको डरे

(God is present everywhere. He will solve all the problems of his devotees. So don't lose heart and never be afraid)

Over millennia we have been conditioned to believe that others are responsible for what we are today – fate, elders, society, culture, whatever. To believe in a saviour is an indication of disempowerment. Empowerment has nothing to do with wealth, fame and lifestyle. Empowerment happens when we take responsibility to shape our own destinies, and discover our true potential.

Empowerment happens when we take responsibility to shape our destiny, and discover our true potential.

Fatalism is also responsible for negativity. This mindset arises because the karmic theory has been largely misinterpreted as supine acceptance of one's condition in life. In other words, whatever is happening or not happening is because of fate. This is how it is meant to be. Therefore, if I am poor, it was meant to be.

The reincarnation theory is an opportunity being given to influence our next life, and is a key concept in Hinduism, Buddhism, Jainism, Sikhism and Taoism. This is unlike Abrahamic religions that do not believe in the reincarnation of man. It is like passing an examination in one shot. You either make it, or you fail. You get one chance only. On the other hand, the reincarnation theory allows one to take the examination as many times as one wants, till one passes and improves one's grades. In spiritual terms, everyone has to pass, and to pass with distinction one has been given many lives. The cycle continues till *moksha* (liberation from the cycle of birth and rebirth) is attained.

The last major stumbling block in being positive is herd-behaviour — there is safety in numbers. Friedrich Nietzsche was among the first to criticize the phenomenon of herd-behaviour as *"the crowd"* and the *"herd instinct."* Just as a mindless mob, a large number of people in society act in one manner at the same time. The logic is that if everybody is doing something, then it has to be right. In practice, it translates into following the footsteps of the Alpha male. Why be different? Why rock the boat? Why draw unwanted attention? In such an environment, initiative is the first casualty.

Environmental Apathy

Despite the explosion of media and the information revolution, many of us are blissfully unaware of what is happening around us, and impacting our present and future lives. We may label this behaviour as environmental apathy – the absence of social, cultural and political awareness necessary to be engaged citizens. Those who are unaware of the environment will also be ignorant of themselves. Most adults are likely to be oblivious of what is taught in a grade 8 text books! If tested, the results can be severely embarrassing.

Many are not proud of their culture; everything seems "to suck." You cannot connect with yourself if you don't connect with the environment in which you live and work. The logic continues; if you do not connect, you cannot realise your potential.

John Donne, the English poet, exemplified the concept of such awareness way back in the 16th century, where there was no word like globalisation: *"No man is an island entire of itself; ...never send to know for whom the bell tolls; it tolls for thee."*

John Donne's message is a proverb in the English language. The meaning is clear; nobody exists independently. We all have to rely on each other as we are interdependent on each other's countries, people, organisation, politics, economics and even the environment.

All of us are bound together towards a common destiny. We must, therefore, know in which direction we are headed. In an interconnected world, to be a world citizen, acting local first is the key for being internationally-minded. Localism means having experiential knowledge of not only one's culture, but that of the people one is serving or living with, their society, their culture, their religion and their everything. This has been a key factor why the militaries around the world find it difficult to defeat insurgencies. Localism gives one a reference point to examine one's cultural strengths and relevance. For any measurement, one needs a start point.

Awareness of one's environment gives a sense of identity and belongingness. The world is a family and we must know where we fit in. Pride begins with knowledge of one's culture. If you are proud of your culture you are likely to be proud of yourself. It is important for everyone to know one's cultural roots, heritage and traditions. Every culture has great strengths and leaders can imbibe them by helping themselves to be good human beings, by unlocking their potential.

Indian culture offers great strengths required for the survival of humanity in the 21st century, as well as creating leaders who will design their future. Regrettably, these signature strengths are not being nurtured through the present education system. Our cultural strengths are impressive; and teachers are expected to inulcate them in their leadership function as role models. Our cultural heritage is rich, and practising one's culture (as long as it does not offend) is an essential part of being international-minded.

India is an inclusive society that absorbed the good features of the Aryans, the Mughals and the British. To absorb the good of other cultures is the bedrock of democracy, wherein minorities and the underprivileged receive their due. Authentic international schools practice inclusivity; there is no cutoff attainment level for admissions. Children with learning disabilities are also accepted. But acceptance is not enough. The hard question put to every teacher is: has there been a significant improvement in the child's overall performance in class and on campus? Is continuous improvement or 'kaizen' happening?

A secular society is one in which all people of all religions practise their faith without fear. The Indian Army is proud of the institution of *Dharmasthala*, a place where all soldiers worship according to their religion of choice. In Sikh units, all non-Sikhs attend the Gurudwara. In Hindu-predominant battalions, all non-Hindus attend mandir services. Likewise, in Christian-predominant regiments, all non-Christians attend church services.

Encouraging intellectual dissent enables acceptance of the other's point of view. This explains why India is the birth place of the four great religions of the world – Hinduism, Buddhism, Jainism and Sikhism. In classrooms, intellectual dissent may be encouraged by enabling 360 degrees feedback on every lesson taught. At organizational levels, dissent is the start point for creating a school and classroom culture, wherein views of the team are taken before arriving at important decisions.

Encouraging intellectual dissent enables acceptance of the other's point of view.

- Employees must be provided with a forum wherein they can express their concerns and suggestions. While the resolution of every issue may not go in favour of an individual, she will at least have the satisfaction that she was given a serious hearing.

- Another classic feature of dissent is learning how to disagree agreeably, a key feature of persuasive communication. Seventy five percent of employees leave an organization because they are unhappy with the boss. Instead of cringing, murmuring and seeking third party intervention, they should stand up and take the bull by the horns. All contentious issues can be resolved across the table in a firm and respectful manner, stating facts, keeping in mind the common goal, and with the overall aim being to clear the air rather than win. Let's remember, a compromise is better than an impasse.

Non-violence is a tenet of all religions in India. Non-violence involves settling disputes peacefully, allowing democratic processes to decide peoples' wishes and aspirations, and finding solutions through dialogue, negotiations and arbitration. In a globalised world that is shrinking in size and becoming more and more connected, non-violence is the only instrument that ensures near-permanent peace and a sustainable world. Indians look at nonviolence as not only a way of life, but as means to an end.

Unity in diversity is a key competency in the 21st century. India is a living embodiment of this principle. Indo-Aryan languages make up 75 percent of all spoken languages in India with Dravidian being 20 percent. While Hindi and English are official languages in the Constitution, there are 122 official languages and 1,559 other languages. Likewise, there are six main ethnic groups, and within them about 2,000 castes. Yet we are one India, however imperfect it may seem to be to the rest of the world.

Leadership Thinking of Generation Y

It is widely believed that Generation Y (born between 1975–2005) have problems with wanting to be leaders. Their attitude cannot be dismissed outright; their mind-sets and points of view have to be understood empathetically. The strategy of the older generation should not be to convert them to "their thinking." Instead, we must get under their skin and try to understand the rationale of their views on leadership. Thereafter, some persuasive talking can happen.

The increasing choices and opportunities that life offers today, as well as the virtual world of social media and computer games, blur our real identities! They are largely responsible for rejecting the concept of leadership. The common doctrine of perceived anti-leadership thinking of Generation Y can be summed up in five arguments. These are:

1. *"I think, therefore, I am."* (Descartes). In other words, I will zealously protect my individualism, even to the extent of glorifying selfishness. In her famous collection of essays under the book title, *The Virtue of Selfishness,* Ayn Rand, the diva of individualism, justifies selfishness or self-interest as morally correct.

2. *"I consume, therefore, I am."* This is the capstone philosophy of the market economy. Milton Friedman, was unequivocally clear on what the market economy stands for: *"The business of business is business."* In this new economic world, money never sleeps, and life is about power, wealth and fame. In the award-winning Hollywood movie Wall Street, Gordon Gekko (Michael Douglas) justifies greed and lust for money:

    "Greed, for lack of a better word, is good. Greed is right. Greed works."

    "Money never sleeps, pal… It's not a question of enough, pal. It's a Zero Sum game – somebody wins, somebody loses. Money itself isn't lost or made, it's simply transferred."

3. Instant gratification; the mindset that I want everything now, this very moment, without delay or deferment. The "pleasure principle" is the driving force behind this psychological model.
4. Leadership is about accountability and that will be at the cost of my personal time.
5. Avoid engaging with problems head-on; over time they will go away.

The second decade of the 21st century is witnessing the emergence of a new type of anti-leadership thinking. We may call it the adventurous or experimental approach to living, inspired by the 2007 Hollywood movie, *The Bucket List*. The underlying philosophy of the experimental approach is that one does not have to be altruistic or follow a vision and higher purpose to be happy. Even pursuing one's passion is unnecessary. Such an attitude is typified in the words of Ralph Waldo Emerson: *"All life is an experiment. The more experiments you make, the better."*

The logic goes something like this. Life is a series of experiences and what I decide to experiment with; it is my choice. I live with an experience for as long as I am content with it; then I move on to some other experience, and then another. The experiments are usually disconnected with each other.

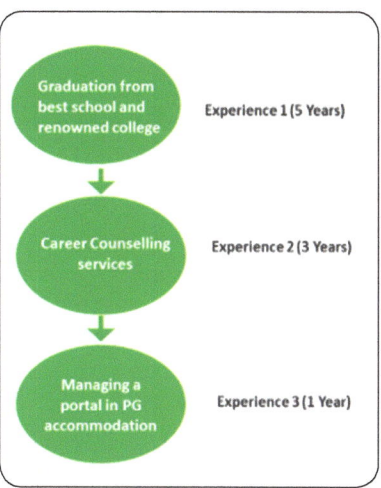

In this model, one does not see the fulfillment of any passion, the discovery of one's human potential, a vision that gives direction in life, or a higher purpose that gives meaning to life. The experimental model is an antidote to boredom, and a narrative of impermanence in career, relationships and lifestyle. At best, it is a desperate search to give meaning to life.

In my opinion, the challenge is not so much about anti-leadership thinking, but developing a new approach to leadership development and training in the 21st century. I don't think Generation Y is against leadership; they are against the present model of leadership being practised by the older generations.

Generation Y is against leadership; they are against the present model of leadership of older generations.

The need of the hour is, therefore, to encourage multigenerational leadership.

Multigenerational Leadership

Today we are witnessing a multigenerational clash – clash in thinking, lifestyle and expectations. In schools, for example, leadership is being exercised by five generations, each different, and each is not prepared to yield ground.

Board Members:	*Silents*	*(1925–1946)*
CEOs:	*Baby Boomers*	*(1946–1964)*
Principals Today:	*Generation X*	*(1965–1980)*
Principals in 2020:	*Generation Y*	*(1975–2005)*
Teachers Today:	*Generation Y*	*(1975–2005)*

Older generations must understand the fundamental principle of change: when you change, the world around you will change. Generation Y is cut from a different cloth. If we want them to change, the current generation of leaders must change first. Our change must inevitably lead to a new leadership culture in schools. That is where the leadership war will be won or lost. This is the bottom line, this is also the start point.

Multigenerational leadership is not what each generation should do or not do, but what everyone should do together by combining the strengths of each generation. The older generation needs to deliberate on the following key issues in multigenerational leadership to find a common meeting ground, and if need be, change the school culture in order to integrate Generation Y with students and older generational leaders. Multigenerational leadership will succeed provided we keep the following in mind:

- Instead of focusing on the weaknesses of Generation Y, let us exploit their signature strengths like loyalty to teams, team solutions, team training, etc., rather than the outdated top-down approach by many institutions. Generation Y are collaborative and desire continuous training and development.
- How can we match their expectations to the maximum extent possible, particularly in respect to work-life integration; praise, recognition and reward for a job well done; and to be explained the relevance or 'why' of whatever they are expected to teach and do on the campus.
- According higher priority for developing their talent in teaching, followed by leadership development for emotional and spiritual growth.

The idea of multigenerational leadership is not in conflict with the time tested principle of traditional leadership. A personal vision, the significance of self-development, positivity and environmental awareness are common to both. Rather, it is based on the principle of "adapt or perish." This is nature's law of evolution. Dinosaurs lived for 100 million years on this planet but became extinct because they could not adapt to rapid changes in temperature. Man's evolution from a water molecule to what he is today would never have happened if human beings had not adapted. In life, it is not the strongest and the fittest who survive, but those who adapt to change and the environment around.

Chapter 8

Goal-Setting

In life, we come across several mediocre persons, and often wonder how they have succeeded in life. Ordinary individuals become extraordinary when they are goal-minded; and extraordinary persons become ordinary, because they seldom write goals and achieve them.

In real terms, goals and plans are relatively easy to envision as they follow a time tested cognitive process. The challenging part is the non-cognitive competencies required to pursue them, such as goal-mindedness, grit, willpower, sacrifice and energy.

Transformation, reinvention, innovation and re-skilling are the buzz; the watchwords in the Fourth Industrial Revolution. Our survival and happiness depends on them. The primary reason why many are unhappy at work, in relationships, and in life, is because they are goal-less and thus lead an unexamined life. The situation becomes even more critical since the vast majority of leaders and managers willingly opt for mediocrity in favour of excellence. They give up easily on their assigned tasks, they look for short-cuts instead of developing the habit of excellence, and are unable to do long-term thinking.

At the beginner's level, the goal is the destination and is derived from a SWOT analysis. However, for advanced practitioners, the journey is the goal, and is inspired by a higher purpose, passion, and vision (or even belief, in some cases).

The Primary Challenge: Goal-Mindedness

Even after conducting several training sessions in goal-setting, there remains a complete lack of understanding of its relevance and cognitive processes involved. I often ask the question: what is so difficult in writing a simple goal and a supportive plan? The reason is clear; about 90 percent of Homo Sapiens lack goal-mindedness, an attribute of learnability. The figure of 90 is supported by several studies on goal-setting.

The best of goals and the best of plans are of little value unless they are inspired by a vision. Goal-minded persons are visionary. The vision expresses the purpose, the why of the goal; it aligns the effort and the intended outcomes; and ignites the necessary willpower, grit and resilience to accomplish the mission, more often than not, in the face of daunting challenges and inevitable failures.

Goal-minded persons are visionary.

With vision as the capstone capability, goal-minded persons have a pronounced disposition towards:

- The unflinching acceptance of the importance of one's self: I am the most important person on the planet because God is within me; and this explains why transformation starts with me. This is not to be confused with being selfish and self-centered in the narrow sense of its meaning. The rationale is: when I change, the world around me will change, and I will be happy. I can make others happy only when I am happy.

- Focusing on the important tasks, the *critical few,* the 20 percent in Pareto's Principle, also known as the 80:20 Rule. Pareto legislated that, in any organization or assigned tasks, only 20 percent is critical. When one focuses on them the effects are 80 percent. By the same token, those who increase their attention to the 80 percent – the *trivial many,* their output is low. Therefore, identifying the critical few and focusing on them is the fundamental skill of goal-minded persons.

- An unshakeable belief system derived from one's experiences of life and work; beliefs based on reason and faith.

- Willpower and self-efficacy reinforce each other but do not mean the same. The scientific name for willpower is volition. Willpower is the ability to resolve and make up one's mind to do something challenging by exercising one's free choice. It is tenacity and doggedness to achieve the mission, come what may. Willpower goes well beyond motivation. Motivation is the desire to do something; willpower goes many steps forward; it is the determination and absolute commitment to achieve something. Willpower feeds self-efficacy to achieve a goal, the confidence and belief in one's ability to achieve a goal.

- Display of high physical, emotional, cognitive and spiritual energy, to sustain one's efforts towards long-term goals, prevent burnout, and be able to stay the course despite all the challenges and disappointments.

- 360 feedback to assure oneself that there is progress and improvement in accomplishing the goal. Feedback helps in course correction when hurdles hold us up, when original plans need changing, and when improving performance to reach our goals. Above all, feedback boosts self-confidence and self-esteem to remain steadfast.

Why Goals Help Us to Be Successful

The primary reason why many lead an unexamined life, and are unhappy at work, in relationships and life itself, is because they are goal-less; and early on in their journey of life, they have willingly accepted mediocrity over excellence. It is, therefore, not surprising that they have no long-term thinking, and are content living in their comfort zone. For such people, happiness remains an illusion.

Goals enable us to be successful in whatever meaning we may attach to health success, business success, professional success and success in relationships. Goals are the mantra; this is the THE relevance of goal-setting.

Success = Economic Value

The 21st century is characterized by the 4th Industrial Revolution, the age of Homo Deus, Artificial Intelligence and machine thinking. The revolution is ushering in the era of VUCA – volatility, uncertainty, complexity and ambiguity. To make matters worse, we are witnessing high-speed acceleration, knowledge and technology obsolescence, the decreasing importance of college degrees, and loss of jobs. There is consensus that, by 2030, about 40 percent of today's jobs will be obsolete. And another 40 percent will be modified to cope with emerging changes and challenges.

Re-skilling (content, competencies and application) will be the order of the day, and shall be voluntary and the prime responsibility of every individual, through informal, non-formal and on-the-job learning. Reskilling is an imperative if man has to have economic value. Those who do not are likely to be consigned to fate, to being members of the *useless class*.

The larger threat humanity faces from AI is the probability that the age of Singularity is near, when the laws of biology will cease, and machine intelligence and humans will merge. And the scary part of this scenario is, in the words of Ray Kurzweil, inventor, futurist, and the world's leading authority on AI: *"Future machines will be human, even if they are not biological."* Kurzweil even predicts a likely date: *"I set the date for the Singularity – representing a profound and disruptive transformation in human capability – as 2045."*

To re-skill, goal-setting is an imperative. To deny Kurzweil's chilling prediction, goal-setting is vital for the survival of the human race.

Success = Effort

In the age of immediate gratification and our wish to live in the moment, in the Now, the value of effort to seek happiness is not fully grasped. Man's deepest regret at the time of death is not whether he could have lived more; rather, could he have done more.

Success does not happen because of IQ and talent but because of effort that goes in to achieve any goal. Winning is a byproduct. Life is effort. Everything good that happens to us is not luck; it is effort.

Effort is the key that unlocks human potential. Therefore, achieving the goal is not important. What we become as a result of trying to achieve the goal, is more important.

The results of a study conducted on students attending the Harvard MBA programme in 1979 is revealing. At the start of the study students were asked, *"Have you set clear, written goals for your future and made plans to achieve them?"* Contrary to expectations, the responses were astonishing. Three percent graduates had written goals and plans; 13 percent had goals but they were not written down; and an astoundingly, 84 percent had no specific goals!

Ten years later the same students were interviewed again, and again, the findings were surprising. The 13 percent who had goals were earning twice as much as the 84 percent who had no goals. But the three percent who had goals, as well as plans, were earning ten times more as the other 97 percent put together.

Effort is sacrifice. Effort is energy. Effort is excellence. Effort is happiness. Effort is success.

Effort is sacrifice. Effort is energy. Effort is excellence. Effort is happiness. Effort is success.

Success = Willpower

Willpower and motivation are not the same. Motivation is liking or desire to do something. Willpower or volition is the determination to do something. Willpower is self-control, fixity of purpose, single mindedness, tenacity and doggedness that arises from one's belief. The deeper the belief the stronger the willpower. Being resilient and having grit to be able to cope with failures is the hallmark of great leaders, and is born out of willpower.

Leaders develop willpower by setting challenging goals, goals that may have a high probability of failure and demand a lot of sacrifice.

Success = Energy

Success does not happen with what one knows, one's qualifications, one's CV. This is knowledge about. Success happens by what one does with what one knows. It is all about application of knowledge. Greater energy and greater passion are more extraordinary than greater genius.

Energy is a mix of physical, emotional, cognitive and spiritual drive. Of this, the physical element is about 30 percent. The important thing is that energy is not finite; it has to be recharged continuously. This is why great prophets, messiahs and spiritual leaders retreated into forests, caves and mountain tops to meditate, to pray, to recoup their energy loss. If we do not regain our lost energy, we will be victims of burnout.

Goals help in managing energy, to direct it towards worthwhile objectives, where it is most required – home, work, hobby and leisure. Leaders, therefore, manage their energy, and not their time.

Leaders, therefore, manage their energy, and not their time.

Success = Empowerment

Most of us do not take control of life; instead, life takes control of us. As a result, we do not know what to do with our lives. Years, months, and hours hang on us. We are disempowered in our eyes; we are afraid to spend time introspecting. We are alienated from ourselves. The greatest challenge is how not to spend any time with oneself, as that inevitably turns into a painful experience.

We, therefore, fill precious hours with strings of senseless activities, along with a heady cocktail of boredom, addiction to mobile phones, social media, and Internet surfing. Craving for social media and a narcissistic portrayal of one's false image, is a cry of loneliness, and adversely affects

Addiction to the mobile phone is no different to addiction to say cocaine and heroin.

mental health. Any separation from our digital companions causes withdrawal symptoms similar to those which an addict experiences when he is denied his favourite narcotic drug. In reality, addiction to the mobile phone is no different to addiction to say, cocaine and heroin. When separated from our mobile phones, we suffer from withdrawal symptoms similar to those brought on by drug denial.

Official statistics in India indicate a dangerous trend amongst corporate employees. 42.5 percent employees suffer from depression, a 50 percent increase from 2008 to 2015. 38.5 percent employees sleep less than six hours when the minimum time recommended is seven. Sleep deprivation exhausts the brain, and over a protracted period impairs performance and triggers manic depression – fatigue, irritability, pessimism and mood swings. It is now well established that lack of sleep over a period raises the risk of Alzheimer's disease.

Dopamine, serotonin, oxytocin and endorphins are the Happy Chemicals in the human brain and are responsible for happiness. These chemicals are temporarily blocked when one is suffering from any form of withdrawal symptoms. Interestingly, the brain is flooded with happy chemicals when we set goals, and put in all efforts in achieving them against challenging odds.

Goals, therefore, empower us to take charge of our destiny, our happiness and our mental health, and give meaning to life.

Selection of Goals - SWOT Analysis

Time and energy in the 21st century are at a premium, and there is no more time than 24 hours in a day. Moreover, the tasks that are to be accomplished are myriad. The stakes are high too: the imperatives of continuous re-skilling, innovation, goal-mindedness, maximizing energy towards priority tasks, and yet being able to maintain a positive balance in life and work. Therefore, selection of a goal is critical, and is derived from a specific SWOT analysis.

Let us say that you wish to develop a competency that will make you happy, or successful, or be able to re-skill yourself continuously. The **first step** will be to prepare SWOT 1 that, will consider all relevant competencies such as lifelong learning, innovation, adaptability, collaboration and learnability. SWOT 1 will enable you to select one master competency from the available menu. For example, you select innovation.

This will lead to the **second step**: a detailing of what innovation means. Why is innovation important to me? Why have I selected this competency over others? At this stage it will be a good idea to visualize the competency, and what your future may look like. If one is not satisfied with innovation, then one returns to SWOT 1, and the process restarts.

Assuming that innovation is the desired competency, the **third step** will be SWOT 2: listing out companion skills for innovation, those skills when combined will lead to innovation:

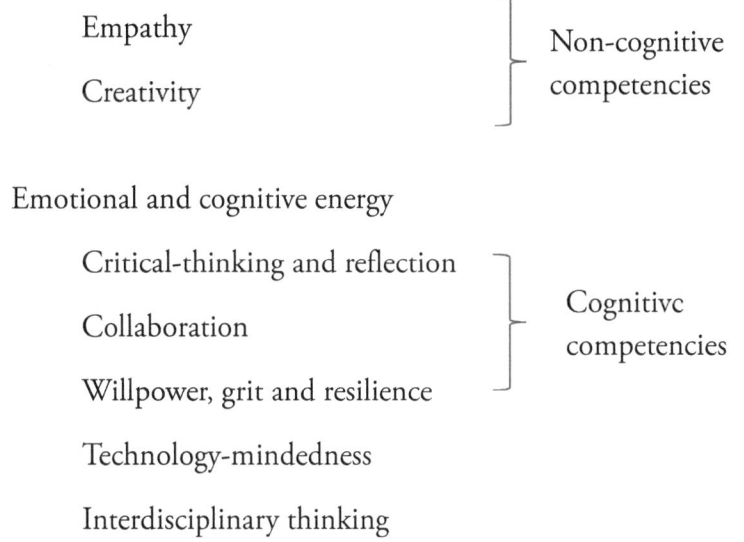

SWOT 2 is decisive as it will determine what key companion skills are deficient, and what goals have to be set. To set two goals with two sets of plans is demanding; and to attempt three will mandate exceptional talent, and high order of energy and willpower.

The Effort is the Goal

Now we are ready to write the goal (s): **fourth step**. The goal specifies with extreme clarity the effort needed to achieve the desired outcome. We often confuse the two. For example, what is the effort necessary to achieve the goal of critical-thinking, interdisciplinary and technology-mindedness? Having considered various options, one may select deep reading as the effort that will enable one to acquire the desired competency of being innovative. Deep reading will, therefore, be the goal and can be expressed in the following formula:

Effort (deep reading) = Final Outcome (innovation)

Let me illustrate the concept of effort with another example. Having gone through the SWOT analysis, I have decided to reduce my weight by 10 kg in six months from today. To reduce 10 kg by a chosen date cannot be the goal. The larger question is: what is the effort required to reduce 10 kg in six months? The effort must be specific, and could be either one or a combination of the following:

Swimming 20 lengths in an Olympic-sized pool daily
Cycling 10 km, 5-days on week days
Jogging 5 km every morning
Gym workout for one-hour daily
45 Day Ketogenic diet plan

My possible goal could be: *I will cycle 10 km on week days and strictly follow a 45-Day Ketogenic diet plan, to reduce 10 kg weight by (give date), with a view to enhancing my self-esteem."*

Effort (cycling 10 km + 45-Day Ketogenic diet) = Final Outcome (10 kg weight loss)

SWOT Analysis

The present format of a SWOT designed by Albert Humphrey at the Stanford Research Institute in the 1960s, has been universally accepted. Initially he produced what was called a team method for goal planning called SOFT analysis, with a view to identify why corporate planning failed. Later, this developed into today's model known as the SWOT analysis.

Although the format is well known, the nuances are unclear to many users. These are best explained by amplification notes on the schematic below:

Strengths	Weaknesses
• Strength should ideally be unique • Leaders leverage strength and manage weakness, unless the weakness can adversely affect your reputation. • Strengths are what others perceive. • Demonstrated consistently.	• Weaknesses are what others perceive. • When in doubt, take a psychometric test. • Character flaw. • Competency deficiency. • Complimentary or companion skill deficiency. • Mental condition, e.g. anger, depression.

Goals Should be SMART-C

After setting a goal, ask the questions whether the goal is:

Specific.

Measurable.

Attainable.

Relevant.

Timely.

Challenging.

SMART goals have been discussed ad nauseam, but specificity is generally absent, and goals are invariably unspecific. Likewise, it is common to note that goals are seldom inspiring and challenging. These two key elements of a goal need greater understanding.

Specific

Specificity arises when there is clarity, conviction and commitment to achieve the outcome. In this regard, two factors will be of great use. The first is in **understanding the Why** – why is the goal important? When goals are connected with a vision or a higher purpose, the effort will be clear, and so will the outcome. When setting goals for a team it is a good idea to get each member write a Why Statement to assure the team leader that the team members are clear about the goal. For example, what do we do (the effort) so that the desired outcome is achieved (the why).

The second factor that will influence the specificity of the goal is the **belief** of the person setting the goal, a belief based on the experiences of life and one's profession and deep reading with deep reflection.

Specificity ensures that the effort outlined in the goal statement is simple, inspiring and measurable. Specificity demands that the goal statement clearly defines the What, How, When and Why. The best way to check this is by visualizing the goal. If the visualization is clear the goal is specific.

Example: *I will cycle 10 km on week days and strictly follow a 45-Day Ketogenic diet plan* **(HOW)**, *to reduce 10 kg weight* **(WHAT)** *by 31 July 2018* **(WHEN)**, *with a view to enhance my self-esteem* **(WHY)."**

Challenging

Challenging goals set apart the high achievers from the average. They unlock the individual's potential and remain focused on the task, by directing their entire energy towards the accomplishment of the goal. We grow taller only when the goal demands great effort. It is the effort that ultimately determines success.

Challenging goals are, therefore, characterized as follows:

- A 50 percent possibility of failure and involve taking calculated risks.
- Place heavy demands on one's energy.
- Involves sacrifice of what is precious to a person – time, work-life balance, resources and commitment.
- Incredible growth opportunities.
- Audacious as the leader takes a quantum leap, as against routine deliberate processes.

Example:

Final Outcome: Proficiency in Spanish.

Goal Option 1: *"Learn Level 2 Spanish by 31 December 2018."*

> The effort is not acknowledged.
>
> Not a challenging goal.
>
> No sacrifice is involved.

Goal Option 2: *"I will work and live in Barcelona for six months from 1st February 2018, to learn speaking Spanish fluently by 31st July 2018."*

> The effort is clearly acknowledged.
>
> The goal is challenging.
>
> Involves personal sacrifice.

Mental Robustness - the Real Challenge

The difficult part in achieving a goal is not writing down a goal statement and laying out a workable plan. The tough cut is mental robustness that is essential for success. The **first** challenge is sacrifice. Most people are not ready to give up their comfort zone and make big sacrifices to achieve goals that are challenging. To sacrifice is to demonstrate one's determination and commitment. In order to succeed in life, to sacrifice is to:

Say "No" to many things we wish to have or to do

Being prepared to give up balance temporarily in one's life

Change one's lifestyle and daily routine

Temporarily give up relationships, should they be distracting

Stretch one's budget to make ends meet

The **second** challenge lies in displaying grit to cope with challenges to attain goals. In the context of goal-achievement, grit implies perseverance or the mental tenacity to overcome failures and obstacles in achieving goals. To be gritty or tenacious is not to quit when the going gets tough. Grit is the result of one's belief that one is on the right mission, a positive attitude, the ability to withstand stress, the commonsense to review progress, and find alternative strategies to continue the mission, and take full responsibility for one's actions and their outcomes.

Before we believe in a goal we must have an idea of what the outcome looks like. The **third** challenge, therefore, is to visualize the goal daily – a mental image of a future action. The logic is: we become what we think – as Descartes said, *"I think, therefore, I am."* Neurons cannot differentiate between what is real or imaginary. When we visualize something the brain sends a command to the concerned neuron to act. The principle is best explained with the example of the *phantom limb*, the sensation 60 to 80 percent amputees experience, as if their limb was still attached.

Visualization techniques are successfully applied by nearly all high performers in every possible discipline; from book reading, to sports, actors, speakers, dancers and leaders. Visualization is a mental rehearsal of envisioning with all of one's senses, in achieving the goal, the desired outcome, and even the key processes involved.

Alpha brainwaves accelerate learning, improve memory, and spawn creative solutions to work in progress. It is best done before and after sleep because at this moment of the day our Alpha waves are at their best. During this phase the mind and body are relaxed and de-stressed, and should be preceded by meditation.

Swami Vivekananda's famous advice to all on success through the power of focus resonates in every strategy, technique, and process of goal-setting.

> *Take up one idea, make that one idea your life, dream of it, live on that idea.*
>
> *Let the brain, muscles, nerves, every part of your body, be full of that idea, and just leave every other idea alone. This is the way to success."*

Chapter 9

Deep Reading, Deep Thinking, Deep Learning

On assuming command of the newly raised 14 Corps in Ladakh on 6 June 2000, I was faced with a fast developing situation of incipient insurgency spilling across from the Kashmir Valley and the Northern Areas in Pakistan-Occupied Kashmir. The red lights were on, and I had to act fast before it was too late. Against all military advice to use force, I recalled some major lessons I had learned from deep studies of military history, politics and revolutions. These were:

a. Political power does not come out of the barrel of a gun; it never did, and never will, especially in the new world order. Rather, political power is derived from popular support.

b. Winning the war is more important than winning tactical battles.

c. The cliché *"winning the hearts and minds battle"* is a shibboleth; to win the minds of the people you have to first win their hearts, their trust.

Armed with this strategy, I launched Operation *Sadbhavna* to win the people into the national mainstream. We achieved spectacular success in less than nine months. There has been peace in Ladakh for the past eighteen years. This transformation may not have been possible had I not been a deep reader.

Such is the awesome power of deep reading.

The purpose of deep reading is to lead a better life, to prepare for an unknown future, and live with awareness, with an awakened mind. To be a better person. At best, reading merely satisfies the reader's curiosity. It is "knowledge-about." On the other hand, deep reading leads to transformation – "knowledge-to be." Regrettably, we have already entered the age of a-literacy, an age wherein the majority of literate people on the planet are consciously exercising their choice not to read.

> *The purpose of deep reading is to lead a better life, to prepare for an unknown future, and live with awareness, with an awakened mind. To be a better person.*

A commission was setup in New York to determine the prison space required 15 years down the line. Setting aside voluminous studies and reports, the Commission arrived at its decision based on the number of 10 and 11 year old children who do not read at all.

In a recent report, 12 to 24 year olds in New Zealand, read 10 minutes a day but watch 140 minutes of TV daily. The National Endowment for the of Arts, an independent federal agency of the US, came out with a shocker. 33% school graduates do not read any book after graduation. Likewise, neither do 42% of college graduates after leaving college. The sad story does not end here.

Even teachers do not read, and are, therefore, responsible for several anti-intellectual myths still being perpetuated in schools, thus regressing child-learning. Some of the most damaging traditional narratives are:

a. 94% teachers believe students learn better when teaching methods match their dominant respective learning style, i.e., visual, auditory and kinaesthetic.

b. 89% teachers believe that people are either left or right brained.

c. Repetition improves learning.

d. Students are accurate judges of what they know.

e. There are multiple varieties of intelligence. Even Howard Gardner is sceptical about what he propounded earlier.

The Leadership Enigma

A man is known by the company he keeps and birds of a feather flock together. Tell me the names of five friends you hang out with, and the five books you have read lately; and I can tell you who you are.

A lot of effort has been put in for driving the leadership agenda in Indus schools: introduction of the leadership curriculum for all students, conduct of 29 leadership retreats, and unlimited conversations; the results have not been commensurate with the huge effort that has been put in. There are two major leadership competencies that continue to elude us, and remain a mystery: setting a **personal vision** and **deep reading.** My diagnosis of this Sisyphus effect, is the presence of low self-esteem in over 80% teachers and students. Without self-esteem it is difficult to have a personal vision or imbibe the habit of deep reading. This is the leadership enigma we face.

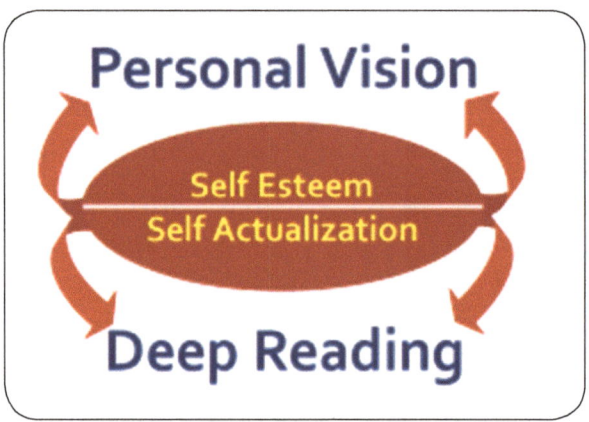

In Abraham Maslow's Hierarchy of Needs, Esteem is at Level 4. This implies that unless an individual has a high quotient of esteem, her self-actualisation will not be possible. The challenge before schools is daunting. Low self-esteem is commonplace amongst teachers, and the prevalence could be even higher than 80%!! The symptoms are familiar:

> Lack of initiative and preference to remain in their comfort zone.
>
> Fear of failure and desire for impact.
>
> Absence of personal goals.
>
> Procrastination and indecisiveness.
>
> Apathy in group discussions.
>
> Tardiness in submission of assignments.
>
> Need for constant monitoring.
>
> Sensitivity to criticism.
>
> Overuse of Facebook and selfies.

However, what gives me a flicker of hope and drives my determination are the profound words of Dostoyevsky:

> *"Man is a mystery: if you spend your entire life trying to puzzle it out, then do not say that you have wasted your time. I occupy myself with this mystery, because I want to be a man."*

What Is Deep Reading?

There is a difference between *reading* and *deep reading*. Whilst reading, a person is absorbing the author's thoughts. In the process, he loses his originality and the ability to think for himself. It is reading for relaxation, for succeeding in examination and at the workplace, for escaping reality, for "knowledge-about." Deep reading is quite the opposite and involves:

> Identifying concepts and ideas, critical thinking to evaluate them with one's experience and that of others, and reflecting on their relevance for the future.
>
> Critical thinking on how to apply concepts and ideas in real-life situations, i.e., "knowledge-to do," or wisdom.
>
> Transforming oneself and others – "knowledge-to be."

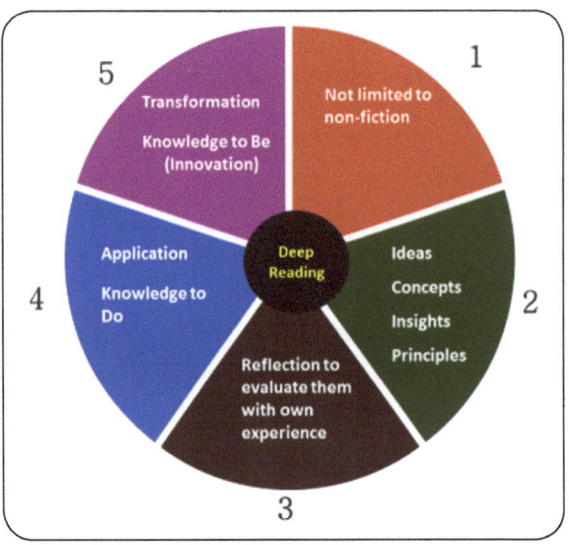

Deep reading and deep thinking are kindred partners, two sides of the same coin; one leads to the other. You cannot have one without the other. The logic flows something like this:

Deep reading and deep thinking are kindred partners.

No deep time.

No deep reading.

No deep reading, no resonance.

No resonance, no wisdom.

Deep reading is not limited to non-fiction books (even some fictional), but also includes articles, journals, blogs, the Internet, digital content, films, videos and documentaries.

Deep reading is not restricted to text or digital reading. It is not a question of either/or; both are indispensable; you need paper and plasma together. You need a bi-literate brain, the ability to balance text and screen reading in a manner that we combine non-linear techniques of surfing the net to find ideas and concepts, and then use text-reading for slow and linear reading to dig down and reflect.

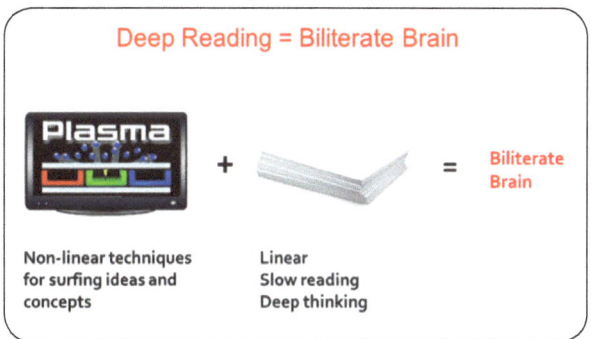

We live in an electronic world, a world where there is a fierce race between paper and plasma. The great media mogul. Marshall McLuhan coined the famous phrase of all times: *"The medium is the message."* According to McLuhan, what is communicated is less important than the medium such as TV, mobile phone, cinema, computer and paper. It is not the content that affects us; it's the medium, the technology. We become an extension of that technology, and willy-nilly technology is coding our minds.

Watch the famous video to see how technology is eroding our minds: *The Magazine is an —I-pad That Does Not Work."* A one-year-old baby from Paris is trying to read a magazine belonging to her mother. Observe how she is trying to expand the pictures and not wanting to turn the pages.

Notwithstanding the obvious drawbacks of being digital, online reading does have distinct advantages that will go a long way in strengthening our deep thinking abilities:

Enables the reader to skim and scan the required information.

Enhanced situational awareness.

An expanded neural capacity.

Self-directed learning is made possible to research as you read.

Easy access to information at one's finger tips.

Carry hundreds of books in a single Kindle device.

On the other hand, deep thinking is the most significant outcome of deep reading, and inevitably leads to the growth of emotional and cognitive competencies critical to flourishing and to being happy, by:

Developing strategic and "big-picture" thinking.

Being innovative.

Finding a higher purpose to give meaning to life and work.

Unlocking one's potential to become self-aware or self-actualized.

Experiencing the mysteries of life.

Questioning dogma and unlearning.

Being inspired to take on great challenges.

Nurturing one's brain plasticity through neurogenesis (the brain creates new brain cells every day).

Deep reading is not to know about; but to do and to be. It is to make ideas and concepts relevant to you. How can they unlock your potential? How can they make others happy? Experientially speaking, the reader's inspiration reaches its pinnacle when unlearning takes place, new learning that replaces old biases, outmoded beliefs and false perceptions.

Above all, deep reading transports one beyond the present world into a state of *flow,* and sometimes into a spiritual and surreal world.

Above all, deep reading transports one beyond the present world into a state of flow, and sometimes into a spiritual and surreal world.

Power of Deep Reading - the Ashkenazi Jews

80% of Jews today are Ashkenazim, a Jewish diaspora population, who migrated to Eastern Europe, and much later to the United States. With an average IQ between 107–115, the IQ of Ashkenazi Jews is the highest in the world, 8 points higher than their closest rivals – North East Asians. In 2012, the evidence was revealing:

- 50% grand chess masters have been Ashkenazi.
- Since 1950, 29% won Nobel prizes, even though their population is 0.25% of humanity.
- With an Ashkenazi population in US comprising 2.2%, they represent 30% faculty at elite colleges/universities, 21% of Ivy League students, 23% of richest Americans, and 38% of Oscar winning film directors.

Why is the IQ Ashkenazi so high? One of the key reasons is deep reading, and understanding the Torah, a religious scripture that is demanding, and intellectually exacting to master.

Threats to Deep Reading

Ten years ago I asked a Grade 9 student why she did not read. Her response sums up the dilemma we face today. She said, *"My father does not read and he is a millionaire. My mother does not read either; and she is currently shopping in Singapore. My teacher does not read either. And even George Bush does not read! So why should I?"* Her message was clear: we do not come across role-models who inspire us to read.

We are seeing the slow and progressive demise of books as we know them – the virtual death of the reading habit. It appears that the death of traditional text-based reading is only a matter of time; and possibly we are fighting a losing battle. It is no surprise that the frequency of reading different book formats even in developed nations is disturbing. Pew Research Centre reported that a quarter of American adults had not read a single book in the past one year. 71% don't read e-books, 93% don't listen to audio books, and 18% never ever read a book. Amongst children the percentage of children who love reading is dropping alarmingly: from 51% in 2015, to 58% in 2012 and 60% in 2010.

School libraries are on the decline. In New York City, school libraries dropped from 1500 in 2005 to 700 in 2014. In the state of California, the librarian-to-student ratio is as low as 1:7000. By the end of 2030, we may witness the end of paper books, with Google, Apple and Amazon as the largest publishers in the world.

In the face of stiff competition from online book purchases from Amazon of today, bookshops are closing down. The phenomenal rise of the plasma brain marks a pronounced shift from paper to plasma, from text to screen reading. And this is where the damage is happening – the switch from linear to non-linear reading, characterized by living in the Now, the craving for instant gratification, the absence of purpose, vision and critical thinking. It is not surprising, therefore, that the educated elite including modern writers, find it difficult to read Hermann Hesse or F Scott Fitzgerald and even contemporary authors.

Capacity-Building for Deep Reading by Teachers

It may interest you to know that the human brain is wired to speak, and not read and write. Language is an invention that goes back 5000 years to the age of Egyptians and Sumerians. Reading too is an invention. In a scenario where the overwhelming population do not read, deep reading cannot happen tomorrow by magic. We have to build the reading capacity of teachers first, and then students.

Three steps for capacity-building are shown below schematically, and are strongly recommended.

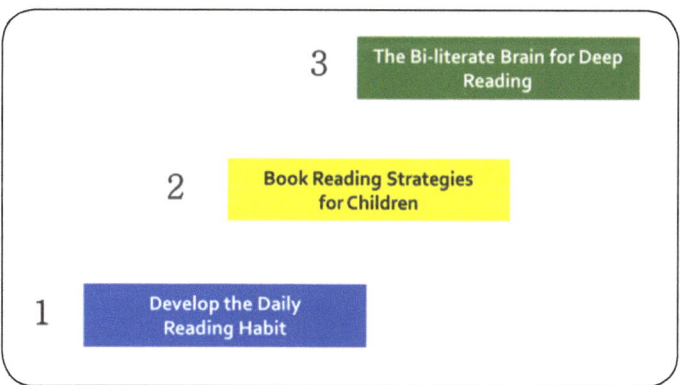

Step 1: Develop the Daily Reading Habit

One of the prime reasons why book reading is not popular with us, is because parents and schools do not seriously inculcate this habit in school. Very few children are read to, and the ability to read for oneself, for pleasure or information, hardly ever develops. It is, therefore, not surprising that later in life it becomes difficult to form the habit of book reading.

Deep reading can become a reality when teachers develop the habit of reading. Teachers are the start point. That is the only practical way to motivate teachers and children to read. To attempt deep reading before developing the reading habit will be a cold start.

In order to be a deep reader, the first step is to form the habit of reading, in small steps. Habits are formed through **repetition** and sticking to a structured **routine**, thereby ensuring automaticity, through strong synaptic connectivity, neuronal recycling, and creation of well insulated neural pathways for reading in the left hemisphere of the human brain. The entire process of habit forming can take up to a maximum of 8 months.. The philosopher Will Durant reminded us that *"We are what we repeatedly do. Excellence, then, is not an act, but a habit."*

The reading habit has to start as early as possible. A sage once said, *"Children who read will be adults who think."* Winston Churchill was even more expressive and prophetic in his commencement speech at Harvard on 9th September 1943, when he said, *"Empires of the future will be empires of the mind."*

The book reading habit starts with teachers and parents. When they read, when they have many books on their study-room shelves in the home, their children are likely to be motivated to read. So, let's start with teachers. The following 5 Steps are recommended for teachers to form the reading habit:

1. Start reading with 10 pages every day for two months; and then set a daily goal of reading 20 pages of a book thereafter. Do this for 8 months, for that is the maximum time it takes for any habit to take deep roots. Once the habit is formed, you are ready to read entire books at a time. Keep a log of what you read, and you may use a habit tracking app like *catch.me*. Logging ensures personal accountability and self-motivation. (Cue cards also help. They can be sequenced and used for cross reference).

2. Always carry a book or a Kindle as your companion wherever you are. Audio books are good company when one is travelling and is not a strain on the eyes. So carry ear phones too. This ensures there are no excuses not to read!

3. Preferably select a particular time in the day to read 20 pages. Reading early after morning is recommended because the brain is primed for learning. After exercise the brain is able to balance the levels of the neurotransmitters which improve attention and memory.

4. Eliminate distraction from the mobile phone by putting the cell phone on "mute."

5. Apart from selective books, read quality newspapers, watch selected videos on YouTube, and quality articles in international magazines like The Economist, Time, Wired and The New Yorker. Quality articles generate interest in reading and develop our multidisciplinary faculties.

Step 2: Book Reading Strategies for Children

Teachers must take the lead in organizing projects involving book reading, analysis and relevance. A student can make out whether a teacher is fond of reading. This becomes evident when the teacher gives an example by sharing her reading experiences with the class. The following book reading strategies for children are recommended:

1. The teacher must read in order to inspire children to read. Her excitement about books transmits itself to children as nothing else can!

2. Teach students on how to read textually and digitally, and demonstrate the benefits of reading.

3. Mindfulness is a necessary condition for serious reading. Right breathing and mindful listening techniques will go a long way in enabling children to focus and avoid distractions.

4. The reading capacity is developed within respective classrooms by setting up classroom libraries up to grade 9 at least, and arousing the curiosity of children by guiding children on the books they should read and enjoy. On every birthday each child could donate two books to the class library, chosen with interest and discretion. Avid readers in a class are often good advisors on new books to buy, for the School Library. Teachers should read some children's books as well.

   Avid readers in a class are often good advisors on new books to buy, for the School Library. Teachers should read some children's books as well.

5. Set-up reading groups in each class, and encourage children to discuss what they have read, and how relevant concepts can be applied in their lives and those in the community. Children must be given the choice to decide on what they want to read. Suggestions may be given from age appropriate published lists, especially contemporary writing, as the classics tend to be tedious for children and adolescents. This will build in student accountability – will enrich socialization around texts.

6. Invite authors and keen readers to speak to children on how they read and follow-up on their reading.

7. At times, movies based on specific books can be screened, such as the The Wizard of Oz or the Harry Potter series. Disney and Pixar produce several films each year, that stimulate thinking and discussion and embed great principles for living, in both children and adults. This will undoubtedly create a lot of interest in reading.

8. Make connections between books they read and issues facing our society and environment. Today, even children's books do not facilitate escapism or the kind of fantasy that does not go beyond narrative. The choice of books is vital.

An innovative approach to motivate young children to read is by inserting a soundtrack in the text. The soundtrack is synchronised with the text, and aims at accessing the inner imagination of the child, while ensuring greater emotional engagement.

Step 3: Creating the Bi-Literate Brain

The challenge of deep reading is daunting. The human brain is not wired for reading. The science of writing was discovered sometime during the 4th Millennium, and all these centuries the human brain has been wired for textual reading. As mentioned earlier, one needs both linear and non-linear thinking to to be a deep reader and thinker.

Schools these days are going overboard in overusing technology; and matters are made worse by addiction to TV, Internet surfing, texting and playing games. As a result, children grow up with **non-linear thinking** characterized by:

> The absence of past and future time. The slogan is clear:
>
> *"I am a citizen of the now."*
>
> Reduced memory and low attention span in the age of increased occurrence of ADD (Attention Deficit Disorder).
>
> Loss of faith in institutions.
>
> Absence of personal and collective vision and purpose.
>
> The habit of skimming horizontally without attention to depth.
>
> Lacking structure, direction, creativity and critical thinking.

Random and often unrelated ideas such as in brainstorming.

Increased emotions with less logic, analysis, and evaluation.

What is desirable is to develop brains which are both non-linear, to throw up ideas and options, and linear thinking to look at the *big picture,* examine them in depth, debate pros and cons, decide on the best course of action, and complete the task in time in an organized manner. Since the brain is plastic, it can easily adapt to both types of thinking. To be creative you have to be non-linear; to be innovative (to turn the idea into reality), you need to be linear-minded.

Developing the bi-literate brain is not as difficult as it seems at first sight. Due to overuse of the digital medium a distinct neural pathway develops leading to specific areas in the brain. A parallel path can be created by equal emphasis on textual reading. Over time, a bi-literate pathway is created wherein two paths are available to enable switching.

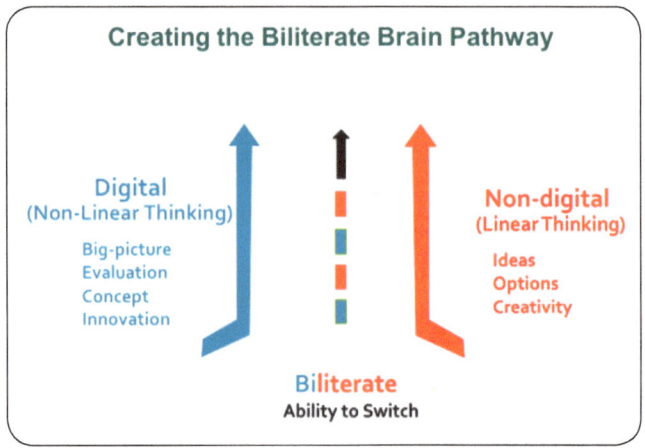

The concept of creating a bi-literate brain is dependent upon several factors – a combination of linear and non-linear reading (paper and plasma), experiential application, solitude, and deep conversation in an informal and social setting. This is explained schematically.

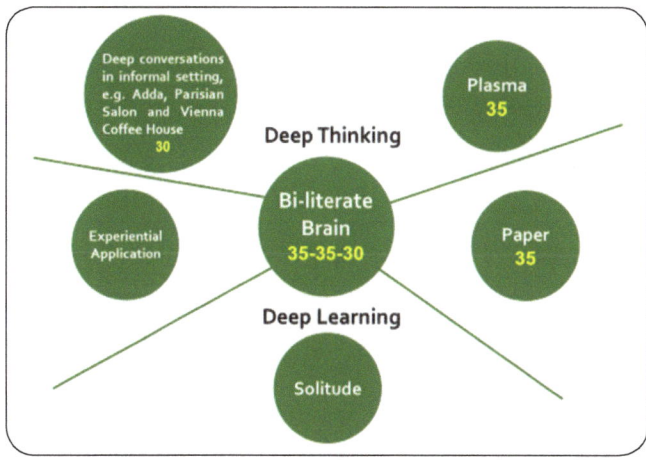

Once again, I stress the importance of both processes in preparing a child to face an uncertain future. This is bi-literacy, a new language of reading off paper and screen, and discussing key ideas and concepts with peers and mentors (for better understanding). A practical time sharing model will be: on line: 35%, off line 35%, and peer collaboration: 30%.

This is bi-literacy, a new language of reading off paper and screen, and discussing key ideas and concepts with peers and mentors.

How to Read a Book

Any form of deliberate reading, or even watching films and videos, requires solitude and mindfulness for deep understanding. Moreover, the reader will need to be skilled in the science of reflection, and the ability to critique. These are prerequisites.

The **first** stage is the selection of a suitable book, internet article or film, or documentary that is most appropriate to the knowledge required. It is advisable to read reviews and critiques from newspaper supplements like the New York Times Book Reviews.

Alternatively, teachers can seek the help of Google in finding suitable reading material. Having selected the right books, a quick glance at the list of its contents, executive abstract and introduction, gives one a fairly accurate idea of what to expect.

The **second** stage that is relevant is the question: how many hours or days or weeks does one spend reading? From an experiential perspective, deep reading will demand a minimum average of one hour per day and 365 hours in a year, or 45 days in an eight-hour working day. This target can be achieved provided you:

1. Reading whenever one has the time like when commuting to work and home, waiting in airports or for a doctor's appointment, and even at work. If Warren Buffet, the world's third richest man, can read 4–5 hours in office, I see no reason why anyone cannot find 30–45 minutes of prime time to do some deep read during working time.

2. Carry a Kindle, a book, or a journal like HBR, in one's knapsack. So a keen reader optimizes reading time to the maximum. One has to read to lead, to learn, to innovate. In the words of the Roman statesman Cicero (106 BC – 43 BC):

3. *"Read at every wait; read at all hours; read within leisure; read in times of labour; read as one goes in; read as one goes out. The task of the educated mind is simply put: read to lead."*

4. Acquire the habit of reading 2 or 3 books at a time, depending on one's mood of the time and day.

5. Re-read quality books (slowly) that are worth revisiting. After every reading, a new perspective and insight emerges.

The **third** stage in mastering deep reading is knowing how to identify key concepts and ideas. The following should be kept in mind:

1. Book summaries like Blinklist and Nat Eliason are not recommended, as they lack clarity on concepts and insights presented by the author. Moreover, they do not stimulate thinking or reflection. With the help of Google it is not difficult to identify the concept or ideas in a given book. But that is of no help. Reading the book is an exercise in improved conceptual understanding, followed by deep reflection. As a result, the concept is transferred from short-term (working) memory to long-term memory.

2. Identify the main concepts, key ideas, principles and insights, and annotate them. If the book being read appears dense and ponderous at first glance; the following pre-reading exercise will help:

    - Read the introduction and list of contents carefully. They are indicators of the uniqueness of the book.
    - Watch a video by the author (like in Talks at Google), wherein the ideas and concepts in books are presented explicitly.
    - Study blogs by reputed bloggers.

3. Annotation of the book followed by note-taking helps in focusing on the concepts and applying them at work and in life. Note-taking by da Vinci (described and pictured in his biography by Walter Isaacson), and the use of index cards by the German sociologist Niklas Luhmann are excellent examples to follow. Over 7000 pages of da Vinci's notes survive. They vividly illustrate:

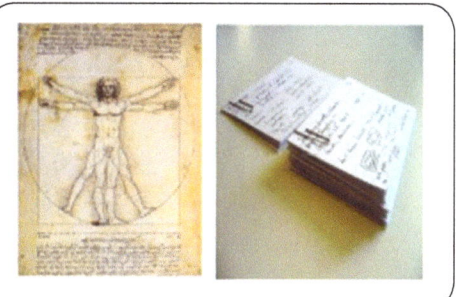

- His creative process.
- Expression of concepts in sketches and drawings. Behind Mona Lisa's enigmatic smile, there are several pages of his studies of lip muscles.
- The famed painter's manner of organizing his notes and diaries. When in his 50s, da Vinci was fearing the end of his life, he, therefore, turned away from painting to organize his notes, describing them as an *"infinity of volumes."*

4. Note-taking is an activity that has been practiced in all cultures for millennia. We may describe it as *creative* note-taking as distinguished from the general purpose or genre used for research and academic studies. Creative notes are not meant for a one-time project but:

- For lifelong learning and creative output.
- Building a research data base for profession enhancement.
- A thought partner for life.

My Biliterate Approach

I have been greatly influenced by the Feynman Technique, an excellent mental model for learning devised by the Nobel Prize winning physicist, Richard Feynman (1918–1988). Feynman often recounted the story of his going into a mathematics class, and challenging anyone to explain the most difficult idea or concept to him in simple language. He said he was able to arrive at the same conclusion they did.

The bottom-line is that, understanding and remembering concepts and ideas are central to learning and efficient preparations for examinations. Therefore, if one is weak at physics, it is because one has not understood the concepts in physics using simple technology. The Feynman Technique can be broken down into four steps:

1. Choose the concept, and write it down on paper.
2. The teacher pretends she is explaining the idea to a new student. In the process she gets to know the gaps in her understanding.
3. Go back to all available resources to improve one's understanding.
4. The teacher simplifies her language and creates analogies to understand the concept. If a grade 8 or 13 year old does not understand the teacher's explanation, it is because she does not understand the teachers' concept.

Ideas and concepts are meaningless unless they have relevance and application in our lives, or we live them out. Even the ever popular Sci-fi books and movies do provide pointed questions for questioning and discussion. That is the challenge. It is advisable to make detailed notes or a mental map, and even re-read the annotated passages for greater clarity and insight. At times it may be a good idea to improve one's perspective by re-visiting the book after the lapse of some time. Re-reading is an effective part of critical reading.

Ideas and concepts are meaningless unless they have relevance and application in our lives, or we live them.

At times the book may be difficult to understand in the first attempt. In such cases it is advisable to read its critical review on the Internet; and then attempt a second try. A book that comes easily to mind is A *Hero with a Thousand Faces* by Joseph Campbell. Let me illustrate this schematically with a personal example:

My Bi-literate Approach:

1. Read Content & Introduction
   Identify key ideas
   Surf selected book
   Slow reading
   Annotation for reflection and Google search
2. Mindmap key ideas for deep reflection
   Read online review for understanding, e.g., *Hero with a Thousand Faces*
   Re-read after a week
3. Digital research – books, articles, blogs, videos, documentaries for interdisciplinary & multidisciplinary understanding
4. Discuss concepts and relevance
5. Application (To DO)
   ↓
   Transformation (To BE)

Deep reading (quite often a combination of text and pixels), as opposed to reading for entertainment or information, inevitably leads to one's transformation – an act of innovation. Deep reading expands the human mind, leading to man's transformation.

Your books are your guru!

For reasons well known, the reading habit in children has not been encouraged by schools and parents. As a result, generations have grown up who do not read. The reading habit is contagious; it spreads like a virus affecting people of all ages. The young are affected more than their elders. There can be no better person

Priorities are the traffic signals on the road of life. Deep reading is such a priority, which only teachers and parents can nurture. In that order.

than the teacher who can set an example in this regard. It is teachers who hold the key to deep reading. Deep reading has to start in schools.

Priorities are the traffic signals on the road of life. Deep reading is one such a priority, which only teachers and parents can nurture. In that order.

Chapter 10

Reflective Thinking

In his famous poem, *The Charge of the Light Brigade* (written after the horrific casualties in the Battle of Balaclava on 25 October 1854), England's then poet laureate, Lord Tennyson summed up the soldier's duty: *"Their's not to reason why, Their's but to do and die."* Courage, death, destruction are the very natural conditions of war, and, therefore, did not merit any reflection! I had been to wars in 1965 and 1971 and saw a lot of destruction, death and misery. There was no time to reflect on these experiences and, moreover, I did not think there was any need to reflect upon them as being in war was a soldier's moral duty.

However, with the passage of time, nearly three decades later, when I was at the pinnacle of *Sadbhavna*, I noticed the transformation from conflict to peace. During this period I read Plato's Apology, which is a recollection of the famous speech Socrates gave at his trial for corrupting the youth, and for which he was later sentenced to death: *"The unexamined life is not worth living."* My understanding of this Socratic principle became clear: It is only when we strive to know ourselves better by reflection, that our life has any meaning or value, that we are able to understand others.

"The unexamined life is not worth living."

In hindsight, most of us lead an unexamined life; and in today's increasing VUCA world which is messy, reflection should form part of everyone's leadership development programme. This does not come without its challenges: we are a most distracted humanity, and we keep procrastinating. We keep putting off reflection for one reason or the other. It is always either *"tomorrow"* or *"later."* But tomorrow never comes; because tomorrow has already arrived.

Critical-Thinking Thought Processes

Reflection is best understood when there is clarity in difference between thinking, reflection, introspection and contemplation:

Thinking is about thoughts that cross the mind, and having an understanding of a situation.

Reflection is part of the critical thinking process for learning, and acting on the outcome of one's reflection. Reflection involves:

1. Thinking about direct and indirect experiences.
2. Identifying ideas, concepts and principles.
3. Establishing their relevance.
4. Application of the outcome of one's reflection.

Introspection is the examination and observation of one's thoughts and emotions, the right and wrong of one's actions (and thoughts), and then acting upon them ethically.

Contemplation is thinking about the future – possibilities, probabilities and readiness to meet the likely challenges. In a religious context, contemplation is a type of prayer.

Think-Time and Reflection

There is a subtle difference between 'think-time' and reflection. The former is a consideration of an awaited significant decision, which often takes the medium of thinking aloud.

Reflection, on the other hand, is a much deeper process that, involves breaking contact with one's daily routine to reflect on:

a. Major decisions affecting the future of one's organization; within the scope of the "big" picture and its implication.

b. Reconsideration of core assumptions.

c. The effectiveness of past decisions.

d. Likely consequences of future action.

Why Reflection

Life continues to elude us because life remains a big question mark. Religion, politics, and reason have no convincing answers. Only reflection has. The urge to reflect arises when one is restless and dissatisfied with the status quo, and there is an earnest desire to know oneself, and bring about change and transformation. Having the understanding of how to reflect is, therefore, very important. This is a skill one can learn with some determined and disciplined practice. Deep reflection enables us to give meaning to life. Meaning gives us:

> Self-identity and happiness.
>
> The strength to exercise moral choices.
>
> A sense of belongingness to oneself, and those we are responsible for.
>
> The time to press the pause button.
>
> An understanding of what reality is.

To be meaningful, deep reflection must become second nature, a habit, a tool to transform ourselves, to give meaning to life, to innovate, to stay alive and happy. Reflection can be triggered by several factors: crucible experiences in one's personal life, what Peter Burger calls *"signals of transcendence";* ideas and concepts in books we read, and impact-events in other countries, that inspire us to transform our present conditions.

Why We Don't Reflect

Given the hectic pace of life and constant distraction, we have little or no time to spare for ourselves. As a result, leaders, managers, teams and employees are unable to focus and decide on matters of importance. A typical snapshot of an office day anywhere in the world looks something like this:

Work (meetings, interviews and mails)	65%
Interruptions and recovery time	28%
Critical thinking and reflection	7%

In an 8-hour day, reflection is 33 minutes at best, if it happens at all.

The challenges that deny us time for reflection are daunting; because of four reasons. These are:

1. The prevailing culture of immediacy and the "urgent." The common underlying belief is that, those who attend to problems immediately, are efficient people. They are unable to differentiate what is important (long-term implication and policy) and urgent.

2. Even think-time at work (not reflecting but merely thinking about a problem or a decision to take) is rare. The non-availability of quality reflection is further impaired because most people attend meetings, seminars and workshops unprepared, and are, therefore, unable to contribute.

3. Multi-tasking is a myth that has been making the rounds. The human brain can process only one piece of information at any given time. To address another task, the process has to stop, before the next issue can be taken up.
4. The oft-repeated catch phrase, *"sleep loss means mind loss,"* leads to cognitive degradation. Sleep deprivation leads to memory and attention loss, thereby impairing the reflective cycle and our ability to judge.

The Reflective Process

'Experiencing' and 'doing' by themselves do not translate into knowledge, or insight and wisdom. Unless we make sense of our experiences and give new meaning to them in life, experiences have little learning value.

Reflective thinking is a critical stage in experiential learning and leadership development; more specifically to reflection-on-action, which occurs after the experience is over, or when it has moved into an advanced stage. Reflection can have many purposes such as problem-solving, decision-making or resolving the moral dilemmas within us. But the greatest purpose of reflection is to be able to lead an examined life.

The greatest purpose of reflection is to be able to lead an examined life.

Reflection is the key process through which an individual can transform and re-invent himself or herself. The process goes through five clear stages: the experience followed by reflection; leading to the formulation of concepts and hypothesis; then active experimentation to affirm the conclusions; and eventually the transformation.

Several people may go through the same experience, yet each individual is affected differently because of their varied cultural background and past experiences. Reflection is a serious process and should be conducted in a formal manner, involving the following process:

- Write down the specific experience and your immediate thoughts and emotions at the time the event is occurring. Keep a reflective journal, exclusively to record important episodic events. Make it a habit to write down the central ideas of every book you read, or meaningful discussion you hold, and then reflect upon them. However, reflections should be reviewed well after the event is over, to gain an objective perspective. To prevent emotions hijacking reason, we should detach ourselves from the experience, and then reflect.

- Develop a new set of hypotheses, concepts and teachable points of view, and match them with one's earlier experiences. Find out whether other people have similar beliefs. Besides, ask your conscience, the inner voice, what it has to say.

- Resolve cognitive dissonance, if any, by either accepting, rejecting, modifying or re-prioritizing the new information being received.

- Experiment with new concepts and invite responses from others on some of the key teachable points of view.

- Gain new insights.

- Transform yourself with a new vision and mission in life.

This is explained schematically.

Reflective Thinking | 179

As leaders we must set aside prime time for being alone to reflect, well removed from daily routine and humdrum life. One does not have to sit in a lotus position to reflect. One can manage to reflect even while travelling in an aircraft, commuting to office and home, or staying overnight at a hotel. Such reflective thinking can be meditative.

How to Reflect

Although reflection is a continuous process, meaningful reflection occurs when it is structured, i.e., a specific time is set aside by making a clean break from work and home and finding solitude – a conscious retreat into oneself, one's thoughts. Unfortunately, most people are afraid of solitude – of being alone.

With motivation and practice it is desirable to be able to reflect-in-action, i.e., when an activity is unfolding itself. This helps in immediate rectification if something is going wrong, or deciding upon taking up a challenge one had not thought of earlier. Likewise, reflection on action is what most of us do – reflection after the activity is over. However, it is only when one has gained experience in reflection on action (after the activity is over) that one can be proficient in both forms of reflection.

The best time to reflect is early in the morning, what sages describe as the *5 A.M. Revolution*. It's not surprising that, all the world's scriptures have been written between 4 and 6 in the morning. In these early hours of the day, there are no interruptions, and the Alpha waves are most active in our brains to think, to reflect and decide.

Alpha waves boost creativity, relax body and mind, reduce depression and anxiety, clear negative and unwanted thoughts, and improve problem-solving abilities. They help the mind to focus sharply. They are most active before and after sleep.

Periodical *retreats* are very useful for individuals and teams to break contact, withdraw into quiet sessions to re-examine fundamental and critical assumptions, and collaboratively arrive at decisions and plan consensually. Retreats have other great benefits. They enable us to retreat into ourselves with a view to reconnect with one's self, an activity that is becoming increasingly difficult in the hyper-paced life we lead. They provide quality interrupted time for team thinking and design-thinking to promote creativity and critical-thinking.

Focus

Reflection demands extreme focus, intensity and mindfulness. With increasing disruptions by digital devices and decreasing attention span, focusing is never easy, it requires hard training.

Nearly 80 percent of our work addresses trivia which does not add any value and is not cognitively demanding. So when we see people as busy-bees, be assured they are awash by shallow work – work that almost anyone can do and requires no reflection. The best habit is to focus our cognitive and emotional energy on less – the 20 percent critical few in Pareto's principle; and act only on what is important (not urgent) at work and in life.

True leaders are independent minded, who have the ability to think for themselves, and act on their convictions. Learning how to think doesn't come naturally, we must learn to think.

A Stanford study on multitasking is revealing, as it reinforces the reality that, multitasking is not possible, that *"the more people multitask, the worse they are, not just at other mental abilities, but at multitasking itself"* (Solitude and Leadership; The American School March 5, 2019; William Deresiewicz).

Multitasking is, scientifically unsound, and impairs one's ability to think cogently. *Thinking means concentrating on one thing long enough to develop an idea about it.*

Focus is sharp and insightful when we don't switch tasks in between. The human brain can process information for decision-making in a linear manner only. Therefore, multitasking is a scientific myth and is like applying brakes suddenly. When we switch tasks we invariably leave behind a residue, resulting in poor performance.

Solitude

Seeking solitude is a ritual in all religions and is regularly practiced by monks, priests and sages. Meditation, retreats and *maun vrats* (self-imposed silence) silence the mind and enable contact with God and one's inner self.

Serving in remote areas as a young officer, and protracted absence due to training exercises, made me aware of the great benefits of solitude at a relatively young age. The vastness and silence of the mountains and the deserts had a profound emotional impact on me. Ever since, I have cultivated the habit of aloneness to be able to introspect and come face to face with my conscience, and continuously review my life. This is never easy emotionally and is the primary reason why many of us don't want to be alone.

Our brain functions best when we are alone. Solitude enables thinking and reflecting holistically, processing difficult challenges, being creative, and re-energising ourselves when we are tired or bored. Being alone makes it possible for me to unlearn – resolve the several inconsistencies and dissonances within the mind – and reconnect with our inner selves.

I was schooled by American and Irish Jesuits, and although we had 'character' as a subject; the significance of the self was never discussed. The concept of self is a relatively modern idea in the West, and it first appeared in the Oxford English Dictionary in 1674. The Western idea of self is individualistic and is closely linked to reason. As Descartes said, *"I think, therefore, I am."* Even Confucianism does not have a concept of self as human beings are looked upon as social beings. Confucianists believe that happiness is here and now.

To be a good leader and an empowered individual, sensitizing people about the self at a young age is essential. Ideas of giving meaning to life through a higher purpose, empowerment, becoming one's own guru, individual self-development, formulating one's personal vision, mentoring, experiential learning, the sense of belonging to a larger community (through community service), and reconnecting children with nature, go a long way in developing the self in a child. All these disciplines require solitude.

The best form of solitude occurs during one's prime time, which is different for every individual. Prime time is time when the mind is rested and functions most efficiently, completely bereft of distractions. For most people it is early morning when our theta brain waves are most active and the brain is relaxed. These waves help in deep reflection, meditation and mindfulness.

Each one of us processes the act of thinking differently. Some allow thoughts to come and go, others pause at stages, and then move on. As for me, I capture the essentials of all my thoughts on a pocket-sized notebook or 3x5 inch cards, and then re-arrange them. The mind does not think sequentially and ideas surface randomly, some closely linked, others disconnected. On other occasions, I take up an idea or an episode or event, and write down my thoughts and feelings, and keep continuing this exercise till I arrive at some satisfactory conclusions.

Seeking solitude need not be a planned spiritual or intellectual activity. Any act which reconnects man with nature also enables solitude – trekking, bird watching, angling, whatever.

Today's and tomorrow's world is hurtling forward at breakneck speed with little or no time to adapt and change. In order to reflect, there is no other option than to press the pause button, to recalibrate our senses, reboot our life and reset our bearings.

Over time we become our thoughts. When we see bad in others, it's a reflection of what we ourselves are. When we see good in others and the world around us, we transform ourselves. Thus, in its penultimate sense, lifelong learning is a process of reflection, unlearning and relearning. When we stop reflecting we stop living for one simple reason: reflection is a spiritual practice. Reflection is not only about looking back; it is also about the future, about perspective, about the most honest feedback one can ever receive about ideas, about innovation.

Chapter 11
Where the Mind Is without Fear

Where the mind is without fear and the head is held high.
Where knowledge is free.
Where the world has not been broken up into fragments.
By narrow domestic walls.
Where words come out from the depth of truth.
Where tireless striving stretches its arms towards perfection.
Where the clear stream of reason has not lost its way.
Into the dreary desert sand of dead habit.
Where the mind is led forward by thee.
Into ever-widening thought and action.
Into that heaven of freedom, my Father, let my country awake.

– Rabindranath Tagore

Tagore's poem, *Where the Mind is Without Fear,* is a prayer in the Gitanjali, for which he was deservedly awarded the Nobel Prize for Literature in 1913. Ever since the Nobel Prize was instituted, only ten other poets have been the recipients of the Nobel, including great poetic seers like Rudyard Kipling, William Butler Yeats, TS Eliot, Romain Rolland, and Pablo Neruda.

This invocation epitomizes the purpose of education – namely, the preparation for life, a long arduous journey in which individuals endeavor to reach their full potential, and in the process, become awakened. In their quest for reaching this goal, they become self-aware. A self-realized person is one who has found an identity, or is at least searching for one. Tagore urges each one of us to strive upwards.

> *An ideal society and an equally ideal person is one that is able to reach her full potential.*

What holds us down are our fetters, our fears, our inhibitions, and our dogmas.

The prayer endorses the reality that an ideal society and an equally ideal person is one that is able to reach her full potential. Tagore describes this poetically by various tags:

> *"heaven of freedom," "tireless striving stretches its arms towards perfection,"* and human dignity when *"the head is held high."*

Regrettably, in today's fiercely competitive and high speed life, full of turbulence and challenges, man is becoming more and more insecure and distrustful, with fears that are often imaginary and perceived. We are suffering from mass paranoia, a phenomenon popularized by media that boasts of its TRP ratings by reporting negative news. This is graphically depicted in a painting titled *The Scream*, one of the most expensive paintings that was sold for $119 million.

The imagery of this painting was inspired in the words of the artist, Munch:

> *"I was walking down the road with two friends – the sun was setting – suddenly the sky turned blood red – I paused, feeling exhausted, and leaned on the fence – there was blood and tongues of fire above the blue-black fjord and the city – my friends walked on, and I stood there trembling with anxiety– and I sensed an infinite scream passing through nature."*

I am reminded of a tourist who came across a beggar carrying a child in her arms. He asked her how she could be happy carrying the child everywhere? The beggar replied that the child was her little brother. The moral of the story is clear: when you don't enjoy what you do, life becomes a drudgery. We have two ways of going through life. We can either take life as an imposition; alternatively, take on life as a challenge. The choice is yours.

> *When you don't enjoy what you do, life becomes a drudgery.*

An Awakened Mind

Tagore's prayer distils the essence of the wisdom of Indian sages. What psychologists like Maslow and Seligman define as potential or self-actualization, Tagore describes it as an awakened mind, a mind that goes well beyond being talented. An awakened mind is characterized by:

The ability to focus on the present.

Compassion towards the oppressed and suffering.

Forgiveness, *"as we forgive those who trespass against us."*

Aesthetics, which allows us to see only the good in bad – in a person, or a situation.

Designing one's life around a set of values.

Universal brotherhood.

The poet laureate specifies four conditions that must exist in society and within organizations, to enable an individual to reach his full potential:

1. The absence of fear through freedom of expression, encouragement of dissent and alternative points of view, and upholding the dignity of mind, irrespective of one's religion or belief system.
2. *Where knowledge is free* and is a fundamental right of every citizen, and is accessible to everyone, and not just the privileged. Knowledge can be free provided a society provides equal opportunities to its citizens, especially the underprivileged.
3. Freedom from *narrow domestic walls* that divide society by prejudices of caste, creed, colour, religion, blind traditions and dogma.
4. Where *the clear stream of reason* has not lost sight of ethics. Tagore prays for the confluence of reason and ethics, of science and faith, of man and God.

Sages, mystics and realized persons believe that the awakened mind can be developed and nurtured through:

Meditation.

Deep reflection.

Servant leadership, by serving the oppressed and suffering.

Doing what makes one happy and enables peak experiences.

Giving meaning to life by seeking a higher purpose.

Awareness of what one is doing, especially one's signature weaknesses.

Re-inventing oneself continuously.

Understanding Fear Is a Function of Education

We are living in an era of paranoia, a deep perception that *"Everyone is out to get me."* A paranoid person genuinely believes that everybody is ganging up against him, that he is isolated, and that there is more bad than good in people. The combination of fake news, an emotive and repetitive media, cut-throat competition, rising stress due to modern lifestyle and loneliness, and increasing inequalities, are fuelling paranoia. Paranoia is an unfounded perception and belief, a delusion that someone is out to harm us.

Fear is the greatest inhibitor to learning, creativity, seeking happiness, searching for truth, reaching our potential and even finding God. Present-day schooling is utilitarian, to place a student in a college of his choice and follow up with a good job. Instead, schools must consider that, a key function of education is to understand fear, and how to be free of it. Only then can an awakened mind be created, only then can creativity flourish. History testifies that authoritarian and hierarchical societies are seldom innovative. This has greater relevance in all-inclusive schools.

The key function of education is to understand fear, and how to be free of it.

The Fear of Failure

Parents and teachers are risk-averse and are afraid of failing. Learning can happen provided it's preceded by unlearning, a painful and turbulent experience. Seeing is not believing because 90 percent of what we see is perception, the remaining 10 percent is reality. The untrained mind has the habit of focusing on perceptions where all our fears reside. Therefore, to think that nearly 90 percent of what we think is failure, is not true. The other 10 percent is *"good"* failure; good, because failure is a prerequisite for:

> Building intrinsic motivation, grit and resilience.
>
> Success in life and at work.
>
> Wisdom.
>
> Self-actualisation or self-awareness.
>
> Happiness.

Parents overprotect their children and insulate them against failure. Consequently, children grow to adulthood short of grit, resilience, and growth-mindedness. The final outcome is failure: they are innovation-deficit. Failure has to be seen as a necessary condition for success. Instead of fearing failure, we must celebrate failure.

Those who haven't failed, seldom succeed. We fail when we don't achieve a challenging goal. In this regard our mindset must change. The goal is rarely the destination, the journey is the goal. What we become as a result of the effort in trying to reach the goal, is more important than arriving at the destination.

Those who haven't failed, seldom succeed.

Failure is good and should be welcomed with open arms. As part of one's training we must not only encourage mistakes, but even set people up to fail (but not become a failure).

Overcoming Fear

Fear of failure is the #1 phobia of the 21st century, and also a prime reason why creativity is being killed, especially in our homes and schools.

Bad parenting is the primary reason for this negative situation. Parents overprotect children, and at the first taste of failure, we see them being overcome by panic attacks. We should be worried and fearful if we are feeling comfortable – a clear sign that, we are not taking any risks, or even attempting to break out of our comfort zone.

Failure - a Learning Experience

We must look at failure as a learning experience, by reflecting on the possible reasons why it happened in the first place. Through reflection and drawing the right lessons, it is possible to use failure to one's advantage. The following three questions will help in focusing one's reflection:

1. *What were the five positive outcomes of this failure?*
2. *What did I learn?*
3. *How can I grow from this positive experience?*

Welcome Failure

All nations, societies and individuals face failure. Those who overcome failure succeed over others. Failure strikes not when we do not achieve our desired goals; but when we give up and do not learn from our past mistakes. What prevents us from trying again is the fear that we may fail yet again. Failure is the price we must be willing to pay to succeed and to be happy. Unless we fail, unless we reflect upon failure, and unless we maintain a high sense of positivity and resilience, success will always remain elusive.

The 21st century is being increasingly characterized by chaos, acceleration, uncertainty and un-knowability; conditions that create some of the greatest fears, and increase the possibility of failure. Leaders must caution their teams that this is inevitable but there is nothing to fear. They need constant reminding that, failure is a part of the process of creativity and lifelong learning. Schools should go a step further by encouraging students to learn from their mistakes; and at times even set them up for failure – allow them to fail but not to become failures.

An easy method to enable a child to experience failure is to get her to set challenging goals with tight deadlines, knowing fully well that it's beyond her present capabilities. Another way is to disallow instant gratification.

Be Mindful

Fear is a product of an untrained mind, a mind that is unruly, distractive and cannot differentiate between reality and perception.

Mindfulness is healing as it helps in re-connecting with ourselves, like an inner disarmament leading to one's moral rearmament. As a result, it increases self-awareness and helps in understanding our emotions better, to be compassionate, peaceful and content in life. Mindfulness calms the mind and enables it to reflect on our worries and concerns with greater clarity and simplicity. A focused and trained mind gives clarity to concentrate more on realities and less on perceptions.

Mindfulness can be acquired through meditation, the ability to focus on the now, and setting aside a 'golden hour' or personal time every day to reflect and introspect. Regrettably, the overwhelming majority of us spend very little time being alone with our thoughts and reflections, our prayers, our aspirations, and imagination. As a result, even when we are in a crowd, we are lonely. Loneliness is always fearful.

Develop a Challenge Mindset

A challenge mindset ensues by setting challenging goals (not within one's present capabilities), visualizing success, and focusing on one's mission.

Given the rising uncertainty in life, the multiplicity of choices available, the complexity of daily existence, and a world that is increasingly distractive, setting challenging goals assumes great significance. The very process of goal-setting takes into account detailing of plans, including possible contingencies of what may go wrong, and how to deal with each one of them. As they say, forewarned is forearmed. Goals, therefore, reduce the chances of failure, as they invariably leverage one's signature strengths rather than weaknesses.

The challenge mindset develops when we visualize success – envision with all our senses. The complete process of succeeding, from start to finish, is rehearsed mentally in the manner champions and high-performers do. Moreover, visualizing life after achieving one's goals is equally important. It is also advisable to visualize experiencing failure, as well as the accompanying feeling. And then visualize you overcoming it.

The glue that binds the champion mindset is extreme focus on one's objective, and not on the likely problems one may encounter enroute. The rule is straightforward: don't lift your eyes from the goal.

Build Great Teams

Why do soldiers die in battle? This is a question that has been asked over and over again. Soldiers do not die for country or flag; they die for their buddy. On the morning of August 13, 1971, Pakistani infiltrators attacked our battalion headquarters near the town of Baramulla in Kashmir. The engagement lasted for nearly five hours. I do not recall experiencing any fear of dying or injury. My only concern was the safety of my colleagues and my soldiers.

In times of danger and crises, strong teams rally around their leader, boosting optimism and confidence, reducing the fear factor, and offering positive solutions. Under such circumstances, teams act as a crisis management unit. A leader's strength lies in the strength of his team. Weak teams create despondency, pessimism

Teams act as a crisis management unit.

and fear. In the long haul, the success of any leader depends on collaboration and the quality and strength of his team. It is, therefore, no surprise that, teams are already replacing individuals as engines that drive leadership and even followership.

Forgiveness

In the turbulence and maelstrom of failure, we invariably come across examples of relationships gone sour. In the final analysis, only those who possess the power of forgiveness can overcome failure. Gandhi often said that, *"The weak can never forgive. Forgiveness is the attribute of the strong."* So the cycle of overcoming the fear of failure is often sequenced as under:

>Welcome failure with open arms.
>
>Reflect on the failure and how it could have been be avoided.
>
>Be positive in your attitude.
>
>Be resilient with great determination to bounce back.
>
>Be forgiving to those responsible for the failure, even yourself.

Most literature on forgiveness focuses on how to forgive others. But it is more difficult to forgive oneself, to exorcise the guilt and evil within us. To move on in life, self-forgiveness is essential.

The great Indian education system unabatedly prepares students for utilitarian objectives of the Fourth Industrial Age – preparation for near-perfect scores in SATs, high examination grades and placement in premier colleges and universities. Such a system systematically degrades creativity, risk-taking, and critical thinking. We are training children and not educating them.

These academic and career goals are supported by motivation through fear. The fear-messages are simple and chilling, and are intended to drive high performance in academics: schools and teachers are not responsible for your poor academic performance of students; if you don't secure high grades, life is over, and you alone will be responsible for it.

It is because of the fear factor, that the Indian and Chinese education systems are not promoting 21st century leadership. Thus far, Indians and Chinese are not in the creative space. Education must aim at awakening the minds of teachers and students, by nurturing their signature strengths and intrinsic talent, and developing the competencies of being good human beings, possessing creativity, critical-thinking, independence of thought, self-directed learning and compassion.

> *The weak can never forgive. Forgiveness is the attribute of the strong.*

Chapter 12

Psychological Robustness

More often than not, there will always be a wide "expectation gap" between school leaders and teachers. In demotivated teachers this can lead to "burnout," being "overwhelmed" and "frustration." In reality teachers and students are never the problem; it is the leadership team. As they are status-quo minded, they pass the blame and the stress on to the teachers, as well as the students.

The success of the purpose of education, the implementation of school vision, the re-roling of teachers, and increasing academic rigour are dependent largely upon the psychological robustness of teachers. The situation is often aggravated by overdependence on just a few teachers, and low levels of psychological robustness. Collectively this slows down the school's efforts in:

- Preparing children for life to succeed in a VUCA world.
- Seizing opportunities to be innovative.
- Developing entrepreneurial competencies to reskill themselves continuously.
- Personalizing learning and making it more effective.

Challenges Schools Face

The majority of teachers have a low stress threshold, primarily because they take teaching as just another job, and not work that creates meaning, or a profession wherein teachers consider themselves as agents of transformation. Surveys conclude that 83% British teachers are stressed out because of:

83% British teachers are stressed out.

- Overload of work and long working hours.
- Professional pressures to meet academic targets.
- Poor student behaviour.
- Conflict with peers and demanding senior leaders.

A deeper evaluation reveals that, as a result of not wanting to come out of their traditional role of mere instruction, there are other environmental challenges that teachers face, such as:

1. Inability to give meaning to teaching by linking it to a higher purpose, which is to prepare a child for a future we do not know, with a purpose, that will endow a child with competencies which will enable her to be innovative, be able to reskill herself, be employable.

2. Ambiguity in understanding universal values and role-modelling them. Core values are spiritual, and a teacher who practices any core value is unlikely to hesitate in pulling out all stops for her student's growth.

3. Decreasing empathy levels in teachers which is responsible for their inability to:

    Personalize learning by teaching, the child and not the subject alone.

    Unlock each child's potential.

Build strong relationships and capacity to love.

Encourage innovation and serve the community.

4. There is a lot to be said about Millennials (Generation Nice) and Generation Z, who are increasingly becoming the bulk of the teaching profession. They have great attributes undoubtedly, but are woefully lacking in sustainable commitment to students. In business language, they are not customer-friendly. They come first, everyone else second. This explains why they are labelled 'Generation Me,' and why they don't like being held accountable.

The cumulative effort of declining empathy, and a lifestyle that is either based on seeking pleasure or power in life, or both, is taking its toll on teachers. The tell-tale signs are clear.

- Although intellectually teachers realise their changing role from teaching content (which Google can do better) to teaching competencies, and teaching the whole child, they are reluctant to prepare for their new role.

- Academic rigour is largely dependent upon strict adherence to systems and processes like daily lesson plans, assignments for self-directed learning by students, assessment "for learning" (and not 'of learning'), student feedback, and personalization of learning. Despite the availability of suitable technologies, teachers find it irksome to be system managers.

- When roles and responsibilities are opaque, it is only natural that, teachers find it difficult to decide on what is urgent and important, and what is their *critical few* – the Pareto's 20%.

There are arguments to support the view that, over time, the transformation in the teacher's role will eventually happen. This is based on the popular belief that change cannot happen overnight, and we must be patient! I do not subscribe to such thinking. Firstly, the rate of change is already awesome, and if teachers do not adapt quickly, they will be overwhelmed. The introduction of AI in education is spreading rapidly, and we don't seem to see the writing on the wall! Imagine, when AI takes over 90% of a teacher's job, and the teacher has 40 minutes to "teach the child," what will she do? Scary!!

When AI takes over 90% of a teacher's job, and the teacher has 40 minutes to "teach the child," what will she do? Scary!!

Difference between Mental Fitness and Psychological Robustness

The reader would have noticed that I have used the term – "psychological robustness," and not "mental fitness." The former does not exist in Google. Mental fitness is cognitive and is a part of robustness. It is a product of the power of the plasticity of the human brain, and comprises:

    Mindfulness.

    Ability to focus on the vital few – Pareto's 20%.

    Critical-thinking.

- Analysis of complex issues and identifying the problem in the first place.
- Conceptual understanding and application.
- Understanding the "big picture."
- Decision-making to include initiative thinking.

    Being self-efficacious.

    Ability on how to learn and how to think.

Robustness, on the other hand, is the synergy of the outcome of an individual's I Q + E Q + S Q + P Q (Physical Quotient). This is shown schematically:

Robustness is the synergy of the outcome of an individual's IQ + EQ + SQ + PQ (Physical Quotient).

IQ +	EQ +	SQ
Cognitive	Mindfulness Awareness of one's emotions Empathy Creativity Grit & resilience Positivity	Higher purpose Meaning Self-awareness Values Beliefs

Robustness synergizes one's IQ, EQ, SQ and physical capabilities.

While "fitness" is a stand-alone word, a part of a larger whole, "robustness" is the outcome of the synergy between all the focus quotients. Synergy implies that the combined effort is greater than the sum of its parts. Therefore:

The outcome 1 + 1 + 1 + 1 = 5 or more and the impact of synergy in school of education is formidable.

1. It inspires learning, an aspect that is vital but has not been written about extensively or practiced in schools. A teacher inspires learning by:

    - Instilling in children a love for the subject; for example, the love for any language.
    - Describing the relevance and the significance of what is being learnt. Why is it important and worth learning?

- How the application of concepts can inspire innovation.
- Motivation to learn and be a self-directed learner.

2. Prepares children to succeed in a VUCA world, by helping to acquire entrepreneurial competencies to innovate and re-skill themselves.
3. Psychological robustness to improve a student's individual level of self-efficacy and academic performance.
4. And lastly, unlock the child's potential.

Strategies for Psychological Robustness
Role of the Teacher

When there is uncertainty and ambiguity about one's role, the individual can never be inspired to give of her best; and as a result, both the organization and customers suffer. Moreover, role confusion can destroy the motivation and efficiency of the team. Role clarity is, therefore, key in the success of any organization. It is now well documented that role clarity improves team performance.

In Vietnam, most American generals and soldiers were not clear, and, were therefore, not convinced why they were there in Vietnam in the first place. This was a major contributing factor for the American defeat. Sri Lanka is a similar story. The role of the Indian Peace Keeping Force (IPKF) was different at different times, and it was difficult for soldiers on the ground to fully grasp the changes.

In the 4th Industrial Age, the greatest challenge schools face is the lack of psychological robustness because of the teacher's confusion about her role. This is not new, as the situation has continued unabated for nearly 600 years, ever since the invention of the Gutenberg Press.

The role of the teacher is to teach the child and not the subject alone – what Google cannot teach. The greatest challenge in developing robustness that we face collectively, is the role of the teacher in the 4th Industrial Age. Despite the Internet, the advent of AI; and the increasing VUCA world we live in, teachers continue to teach content! Why don't we realize that we are doing irreparable damage to ourselves and future generations by teaching content? Why don't teachers realise that they are no longer the sole repositories of knowledge.

The role of the teacher is to teach the child and not the subject alone.

The greatest challenge is not that teachers do not understand what their new role is, and why it is inevitable. The challenge is, that they have to retrain themselves completely – a Herculean task! As long as there is either role confusion or role inadequacy, and inadequate psychological robustness within teachers, schools will not be able to prepare children for the 21st century challenges.

Identify Potential Leaders

The second strategy is to identify potential leaders within teachers. Potential is aptitude that can be transformed into talent by mentoring, coaching, and providing experiential opportunities to grow. This is not easy because school leaders often confuse potential with performance. Performance is what one does, and potential is what one could do. Another big mistake that is common is that an individual's leadership potential is judged upon her current managerial performance. In the armed forces, an excellent unit commander may not make an equally excellent general! Likewise, an excellent manager may not make an equally excellent CEO. The job requirements are different.

An excellent manager may not make an equally excellent CEO. The job requirements are different.

Teachers who possess the desired potential, are likely to display the following indicators, (although presently they may not hold leadership positions).

- Are intrinsically motivated to learn and work hard to get the job done. Do they have the aspirations to tackle opportunities, and aspire for greater responsibilities and autonomy of a specific leadership position within the organization.
- Team players who realize that no single person has all the answers because of the complexities of the challenges we face.
- Demonstrate the capability of coping with stress, through positive mental attitude (PMA).
- Can role model at least a few of the school's core values, if not all.
- Are they goal-oriented?

Identifying potential is a competency senior leaders need to develop, and be judged on as part of their evaluation. Unless this capability is acquired, nurturing talent will not be possible.

Create 2nd Rung of Leadership @ All Levels

"Insider First" should always be the hiring preference. Insider promotions are favoured over importing teachers, because the former understand the culture of the school, its values, ethos and expectations. In reality, it's only when a person serves under you, is it possible to see her true worth. Even the best of CVs may not be indicative of a teacher's true potential.

The prime responsibility of school leaders is to inspire and develop next generation leaders. School leaders are expected to give this responsibility their personal commitment, and should be prepared to give about 25 percent of their time and energy towards their objective.

Creating the 2nd rung of leadership is a key element of the school leaders' critical few – his/her 20 percent. Those selected should be capable of thinking 2-up and acting 1-up. This is possible provided school leaders:

- Share their intent of their *"critical few"* down with ALL teachers.
- Focus on self-growth as a prerequisite for professional development.
- Spend 25 per cent of their time in nurturing talent.

Nurturing Talent

Nurturing one's own talent is the 1st priority. Nurturing a teacher's talent is 2nd priority.

Nurturing talent is usually associated with a leadership promotion. If we want to institutionalize a school, we must also consider creating a pool of varied talent such as "master teachers" and "teacherpreneurs," as new career options on parallel track. While the latter raise the academic bar, the former help in innovation and transformation of education.

Nurturing talent requires a team of trainers drawn from the common talent pool. These trainers should work under the Principal and mentor the talent team in the fundamentals of:

Psychological robustness.

Deep reading.

Innovation.

Goal-setting.

Artificial Intelligence.

Re-skilling.

Pareto's 80/20 Principle

A fair number of teachers remain unproductive as they are unable to select and focus on their critical few – the 20%. Consequently, they end up frustrated and stressed out. Successful leaders never lift their eyes from their 20% – their goal, their key result areas. If a detailed analysis of a school leader's daily routine in school is done, it will not be surprising to find that most are not spending 80% of their time on the 20% critical few! We are drowned in a sea of details.

By disciplining oneself to identify (not easy) and focus on what is important and not urgent (the critical 20%), a leader's productivity and motivation goes up substantially. Principals and Heads of Schools must help teachers to identify their 20, insist on individual plans, review them continuously, ensure vertical and horizontal alignments, and also role model Pareto's Principle.

Challenging Goals

Challenging goals raise the quality of learning and student-teacher motivation. They unlock one's potential. A challenging goal is a goal that:

- Is beyond one's present capabilities, and it's very likely that one is not 100% certain of achieving it.
- Has a 50% probability of failures, and involves high risks.
- Inevitably, it places demands on sacrificing what is precious to a person.
- Requires innovative solutions.
- Is interdisciplinary in nature.

The Champion's Mind - One Step Beyond By Robustness

It is not enough to be psychologically robust; we must go one step forward to develop the champion's mindset. Champions think gold, not silver. As Muhammed Ali once said, champions *"have a desire, a dream, and a vision."* Gold is, therefore, the colour of excellence – in oneself, and in others, because the champion's mindset is wired to win, to succeed, and to inspire. Champions are outliers; and they achieve this distinction by:

- Leading first; teaching second.
- Possessing a strong belief in themselves and the strength of a higher power – self-efficacy; the belief in one's ability to achieve one's goals.
- An intense burning focus on their goals.
- Being resilient: *"Fall down seven times and stand up eight."* (Japanese proverb).
- Being concept-minded.
- Proficiency in entrepreneurial competencies to reskill themselves continuously.
- Discipline – mind over matter.
- Competing with themselves, not others.
- Deep reading to gain insight and wisdom.

Conclusion - Inner Strength, the Final Step

The journey of mind over matter is the journey of mental fitness, then psychological robustness; and ultimately inner strength.

The power of inner strength is based upon:

A higher purpose that gives meaning to life.

Peace within – not allowing others to control our emotions, because I am the most important person in my life.

To accept and love life as it is; not what it should be.

To lead an examined life, because an unexamined life is not worth living.

Creativity – the ability to continuously reinvent oneself, to be reborn.

The universal values of empathy, love, respect and discipline.

Do not seek God in your temples or religious dogma – seek God within you.

Afterword – What Google Should Teach

The 4th Industrial Revolution is already making deep inroads, not only into business, politics and the environment, but even in the life of the common man. The revolution is characterized by Artificial Intelligence, machine-thinking, volatility, uncertainty, complexity and ambiguity, or VUCA. The challenges for humanity are daunting: to benefit from the rewards of Artificial Intelligence, to make the world a better place to live, and to infuse the absence of fear – a prerequisite for innovation, economic growth, happiness and social equity.

There are genuine concerns about authoritarianism and mind-bending propaganda tools; threats to transparency and accountability, ethical dimensions in innovation; the possible loss of purpose; a crumbling education system; fears amongst the minorities and migrants; and the perceived rich-poor divide.

The need of the hour is the absence of fear.

We need constant reminding that, in the long haul, future competition will not be between conflicting political ideologies and competing economic systems, but between contending education systems. Education alone can combat the paranoia of Armageddon-like scenarios arising from the advent of Artificial Intelligence. Ever since the invention of the Gutenberg printing press in 1440, education has focused on controlling the outer world. This explains the demise of liberal education; our fetish for science, mathematics, standardized testing; one-shoe-fits-all delivery of academics, and targets for high scores in examinations. This approach is horribly flawed, but the legacy continues unabated.

In the 4th Revolution, knowledge, jobs and technology are becoming obsolete at an alarmingly high rate. By the time a child in grade 1 graduates from school, nearly 42 percent of today's jobs will have disappeared. Of the remaining 58 percent, nearly 50 percent will be refashioned to meet the needs of the changing times. Consequently, continuous re-skilling will be the order of the day. Those who lack innovative intelligence will be socially disadvantaged and emotionally challenged. They will have no political or economic value, and this will inevitably lead to dissatisfaction and civil disobedience, as well as greater social and economic disparities.

Though we cannot compete with machines and algorithms, the only effective way we can outmatch them is by expanding the human consciousness; through purpose, vision and servant leadership, by accessing our inner world, the world of thoughts, feelings and emotions; and by purging our fears. Innovation is the number one leadership and spiritual competency. Therefore, education must erase the present distinction between leaders and managers; that is an outdated concept. Everyone is a leader. Only great leaders can be conscious citizens, value-driven parents, effective teachers and great human beings.

Learning cannot happen in an environment where making mistakes is discouraged, where the zero-error syndrome hangs like the sword of Damocles, or situations where questioning by citizens is seen as dissidence. Even though this may appear to be a flawed perception, the reality is that we are living in a world of fake news and paranoia. A paranoid person genuinely believes that *"Everyone is out to get me."* The cocktail of fake *news,* an emotive and repetitive media, cut-throat competition, and the rising stress of acceleration in our lifestyles, increases inequalities and engenders loss of opportunities.

Fear is the greatest inhibitor to learning, to innovation, to progress, to happiness, in fulfillment in reaching our potential, and even finding whichever God we believe in. Present day schooling is utilitarian – the development of Economic Man rather than Moral Man. Schools and institutions of higher learning must consider that, a key function of education is to understand fear, and how to be free of it. Only then can a mind be awakened; only then can innovation flourish.

This is the fear the current and future world faces.

The India Nobel laureate and poet, Rabindranath Tagore's poem, *Where the Mind is Without Fear,* must resonate with every citizen. The poem cannot be dismissed as a utopian idea, simply because it visualizes a world where people are not afraid to dissent, and express their ideas freely and without fear.

This is the awakening humanity requires and Rabindranath Tagore still matters. Education must ensure that his ideals of human freedom live on:

> *"Where the mind is without fear and the head is held high where knowledge is free where the world has not been broken up into fragments by narrow domestic walls."*

This is the moral rearmament that is overdue – to live with respect, dignity, and without fear. This is possible only through education, education of the heart and the mind, and not the head alone – education that will transform peoples' apathy into hope.

This is the freedom we are seeking – freedom from fear.

Can Google do this?

CPSIA information can be obtained
at www.ICGtesting.com
Printed in the USA
LVHW072105050222
710380LV00011B/40